THIS IS US

Life Together in God's Family

Trinity Lutheran Church

Copyright © 2017 Trinity Lutheran Church, Lisle, IL
All rights reserved.

CONTENTS

Attributions/Bible Versions Used iv

TRINITY FAMILY VALUES v

THIS IS US INTRODUCTION 1

WEEK 1 WE ARE A GROWING FAMILY 6

WEEK 2 WE GO WHERE THE SPIRIT LEADS US 17

WEEK 3 GOD DOES AMAZING THINGS THROUGH US 29

WEEK 4 WE TAKE RISKS FOR THE GOSPEL 41

WEEK 5 SOMETIMES WE DON'T GET ALONG 52

WEEK 6 WE WELCOME ALL 64

WEEK 7 WE GIVE SACRIFICIALLY 75

WEEK 8 WE REACH OUT WITH THE GOOD NEWS 88

VIDEO NOTES ANSWER KEY 99

LEADER NOTES 101

APPENDIX 111

We thank these wordsmiths for using their gifts for the Body of Christ at Trinity:
Eric Gradberg for the session closing prayers;
Marge Franzen, Greg Placko, Jenny Price and Mark Schulz
for the *Today's Text* streams.

BIBLE VERSIONS USED

Amplified Bible (AMP)
Copyright © 2015 by The Lockman Foundation, La Habra, CA 90631. All rights reserved.

Contemporary English Version (CEV)
Copyright © 1995 by American Bible Society. All rights reserved.

English Standard Version (ESV)
The Holy Bible, English Standard Version. ESV® Permanent Text Edition® (2016). Copyright © 2001 by Crossway Bibles, a publishing ministry of Good News Publishers.

The Good News Translation (GNB)
Copyright © 1992 by American Bible Society.

GOD'S WORD Translation (GW)
Copyright © 1995 by God's Word to the Nations. Used by permission of Baker Publishing Group.

The Message (MSG)
Copyright © 1993, 1994, 1995, 1996, 2000, 2001, 2002 by Eugene H. Peterson.

New Century Version (NCV)
The Holy Bible, New Century Version®. Copyright © 2005 by Thomas Nelson, Inc. Used by permission. All rights reserved.

New International Version (NIV)
The Holy Bible: New International Version. (1984). Grand Rapids, MI: Zondervan.

New Living Translation (NLT)
Holy Bible, New Living Translation, copyright © 1996, 2004, 2015 by Tyndale House Foundation.

The Living Bible (TLB)
The Living Bible copyright © 1971 by Tyndale House Foundation.

Map (page 19) from *The Lutheran Study Bible* © 2009 Concordia Publishing House. Reproduced by permission under license number 17:07-04B

TRINITY'S FAMILY VALUES

These are the behaviors that reflect what it means to be an ideal family member. We ask everyone who is a part of Trinity to live out these values. No family is perfect and we recognize that we are all growing, but being in the family means we are all working towards this ideal.

Worship—We worship weekly, whenever possible.
Weekly public worship at one of our sites is a high priority in our lives. If you can be there, you are there.

Connect—We are in small group communities.
Those small groups are healthy, meaning they study the Word, are coached in and connected to Trinity's mission, and meet regularly.

Serve—We serve regularly in a ministry at Trinity and in our local communities.
We seek to know our gifts and use them for the sake of others. We serve the Trinity community and our local communities either through a Trinity ministry or on our own.

Generosity—We tithe or give beyond a tithe.
Tithing is giving 10% off the top. But being generous is about more than a minimum percentage. It means we are also open to being generous whenever God gives us an opportunity to do so.

Leading—We are willing to be led and to use our gifts to lead others.
Everyone needs the support, encouragement, and accountability that comes from being led. But it also means becoming a leader for the sake of serving others.

Sharing—We intentionally cultivate and have relationships with at least two people who are far from God.
We all have people in our lives who don't yet follow Jesus. Committing to sharing means we are actively praying for them, inviting them to church, and having regular spiritual conversations with them.

Accountability—We are willing to be held accountable for our own growth and leadership by others within the church family.
Accountability means that we are willing to follow through on our commitments and receive the support and encouragement from others to do so. It means being transparent with those in our small group communities and our leadership teams about what is going on in our lives and where we could use encouragement and support.

THIS IS US   INTRODUCTION

LET ME INTRODUCE YOU

I page through the family album. Faces look back at me with a familiar curve to the smile. A nose appears generation after generation. Pictures of infants are somewhat confusing. I long for a passed generation to explain. In the background are surroundings, some strange, some familiar. "Look how small the big maple was!" "Remember Grandma's fishpond?" "Where were they?" "Who's that standing next to them?"

Trinity has had a long family life, too. It's full of snapshots; a group meeting with the District Mission Director, a shovel of dirt, an A frame, big dream projects, church in a trailer, an empty Walgreens, marketplace daycare, urban mission. Paging rapidly through old pictures and new snaps can be confusing. Who were they? Who are we? Is it me here and them there—or is it all us?

The Acts of the Apostles is a family album, too. We see snapshots of the early church as the Holy Spirit moves them through the mission Jesus had entrusted to them. We're looking at 16 stories that serve to remind us of who they were, the people first trying to figure out what "church" was to be. We also learn more about who we are, driven by the same Holy Spirit on the same mission to look, live and love more like Jesus and help others to do the same.

The 16 stories in this series are arranged as eight pairs, one on Sunday and one for your group session. Though not chronological, the two will connect and feed each other, so encourage each other to not miss a single weekend and to review the sermon by listening to the audio file posted at TLC4u.org/sermons.

Looking at that old picture album often makes me wonder what's next? What new faces will be appearing on the following pages? Each session builds a plan for movement on that question. We want you to feel the Holy Spirit's nudge as he breathes in you with these snapshots from Acts. We want you to see new faces that could be added to the family album. Help each other be specific in these conversations. Support each other in making plans so that more people can say, "This is us!"

TRINITY FAMILY VALUES

You'll find a listing of Trinity's Family Values on page v. They have been developed to help us clarify the traits that appear in all of Trinity. They describe our family resemblance. Certain values will also appear in a picture frame within sessions two through eight. This serves as a family snapshot for the session. We included them to give you a glimpse of what you'll be hearing in your conversation during the session. Listen for how that value plays out in our individual, group, and congregational life, especially considering the session's theme.

WORSHIP AND PRAYER

The book of Psalms was a combination hymn book and prayer book for the Judaic community in our first century AD setting for the book of Acts. The early church that we see in formation would be using that tool steadily in their private worship and when they gathered in the Temple for worship. With that in mind we've selected eight psalms for you to use in your group worship time. A variety of formats are suggested inviting people to voice a prayer or a testimony, but please use your gifts and the gifts of others in your group to explore the limitless way these prayers and songs of praise can be used. You may already have an established practice and comfort zone or you may need to establish one. Don't fear a stretch. Stretching a muscle brings both healing and growth, so try something new.

Groups often have a habit of opening or closing by collecting prayer requests. Rather than have a designated time, you'll find some of this happening naturally in the opening worship or closing prayer and throughout the session. Each week's session has a **Prayer Notes Page** where you can be taking notes throughout the session.

Each week's session will conclude with a responsive prayer time that encapsulates the study, the video message and the psalm for the week. The prayer is divided into leader and group responses. That leader role can be shared among the group over the series. As you read through the call and response format, set a slow meditative pace. As you become familiar with the format you can also tuck in specific personal or group prayers.

Your practice of worship and prayer is one way you acknowledge the presence of our Lord Jesus in your group. After the resurrection, we have several accounts of Jesus physically appearing to disciples gathered together. After some interaction, he is suddenly gone. Repeatedly, accounts are given of *here* then *gone*. The Gospel of Matthew closes with a final here/gone account with the promise to "be with you always." It seems the disciples are gradually developing a comfort zone of knowing Jesus is present even without his physical body in the room. Use your worship and prayer time to say, "Jesus is here!" He's part of your conversation. He's guiding your discussion. He's listening to your personal pain and the commitments you make. Discuss together if having a "Jesus Chair" in the room would help you with this awareness. Pause at any point in your session discussions to address Jesus in prayer and ask for his Spirit's guidance. If someone in your group has the spiritual gift of prayer give them license to call for a prayer timeout anywhere in the session. Some have been written in for you. With practice, others in the group will also grow this sensitivity for the need to talk to Jesus together.

THE STUDIES

We have provided a video introduction to each story you'll be unpacking in Acts as well as background details and some discussion strategies. Videos are available on DVD or can be streamed from TLC4u.org/ThisIsUs. We want these conversations to deepen your understanding of God and his desire for the whole world. We also want you to deepen your understanding of each other, to grow into a Trinity Family relationship. Honor each other when a personal story is shared. Look for application and links in God's Word that may show someone their next step in God's grace. Bring other resources in that meet the needs and minds in your group. Add questions… skip questions… each group is a unique combination of people, surroundings, and space of time, so make the study fit the group.

You will notice an occasional emoji popping up in the videos and the group session material. Your reaction may be, "What?!?!?!!!?" We want your group's interaction to be transparent. A certain level of vulnerability will be deep soil for growth. So, we want to acknowledge and even invite emotional responses that come from reading God's Word and interacting together. We offer these graphics as a little salt and pepper in the recipe for your group time. Let them spark discussion or even contradiction, but don't let them become a distraction. Add more or less to your own taste. 😃

TODAY'S TEXT

Your time together as a group will be loaded with connecting the dots. Your discussions will jump from the first century to the twenty-first century. In between sessions, we invite everyone into a spiritual discipline of meditation and reflection with *Today's Text*. This is a time to hear God's Word and see what he is pointing out in your own attitudes and actions. This is where you open your heart to the change that the Holy Spirit is working to make you more like Jesus. Yes, your schedule is overbooked, but working *Today's Text* stream is an opportunity to honor God with an appointment five days a week for eight weeks. Give him the time. He will not disappoint.

GROUP SERVE

As you can see from our Family Values, serving is an important component in our life at Trinity and in your life as a small group. Serving together is a powerful way to get to weave your lives together. Serving in the community opens your eyes to see God's mission all around you. Your group serving plans also offer a great opportunity to bring family and friends into action and often opens doors for a new level of conversation. Planning some way to serve together is a key aspect of being able to say *This Is Us*.

We have an exciting serving option for you. Trinity is joining forces with other congregations and Feed My Starving Children for a Western Suburb *Live the Love* mobile pack event, November 4 at the Odeum Expo Center in Villa Park. Your group has the opportunity to join in the pack and also join in the funding for the food and the shipping expense. #feed100kidsforayear! Start exploring your options early. Registration will open October 1, so book your group early. Especially encourage everyone to use this as a way to involve friends and family not in your group. People like to make an impact in the lives of under-resourced children and it's a perfect opportunity for them to rub elbows with your group. To understand more about the mission of Feed My Starving Children go to www.fmsc.org. To find out more about the *Live the Love* pack and registration, go to www.tlc4u/makeadifference. To donate, go to https://give.fmsc.org/LiveTheLove

Finally—We want our church to be a family that loves and cares, challenges and encourages and reaches to impact other lives. We are praying that these next eight weeks will help us learn more and more to be there for one another. To learn what it means to be God's family. We're praying for you as individuals and as a group as you begin this journey together. And we're praying that this fall will be a time that we all look back on some day and say—that's when God really made us a big, wonderful, growing, joyful family! ☺

WEEK 1 WE ARE A GROWING FAMILY
Acts 2:42–47

WORSHIP

Psalm 30

Put yourself in the place of a disciple having witnessed Jesus' death and resurrection, then reciting this psalm in the Jerusalem temple for a time of prayer and worship. Can you bring their joy 😊 and excitement into your voice as you read Psalm 30 together?

Psalm 30 (NCV)

> $^{30:1}$ I will praise you, L ORD,
>> because you rescued me.
>> You did not let my enemies laugh at me.
>
> ^{2} L ORD, my God, I prayed to you,
>> and you healed me.
>
> ^{3} You lifted me out of the grave;
>> you spared me from going down to the place
>> of the dead.
>
> ^{4} Sing praises to the L ORD, you who belong to him;
>> praise his holy name.
>
> ^{5} His anger lasts only a moment,
>> but his kindness lasts for a lifetime.
>> Crying may last for a night,
>> but joy comes in the morning.
>
> ^{6} When I felt safe, I said,
>> "I will never fear."
>
> ^{7} L ORD, in your kindness you made my mountain safe.
>> But when you turned away, I was frightened.
>
> ^{8} I called to you, L ORD,
>> and asked you to have mercy on me.
>
> ^{9} I said, "What good will it do if I die
>> or if I go down to the grave?
>> Dust cannot praise you;
>> it cannot speak about your truth.

>¹⁰ LORD, hear me and have mercy on me.
>   LORD, help me."
>
> ¹¹ You changed my sorrow into dancing.
>   You took away my clothes of sadness,
>   and clothed me in happiness.
>   I will sing to you and not be silent.
>   LORD, my God, I will praise you forever.

Acts 2:42 –47

Have someone in your group read the text while everyone listens and leave a silent space for internal processing of what has been heard. People may want to open their Bible and underline a word or phrase that stands out, but save the discussion for later.

VIDEO

Notes:

Being part of the family can be ___*frustrating*___.

"___*Family*___" is one of the main ways that God describes his church.

People sharing their ___*hearts*___

They loved each other because ___*Jesus told them to*___

_____.

DISCUSSION

It is clear in the Acts 2 account that people who have heard the Gospel and been touched by the Holy Spirit respond by making commitments. Your personal experience of family commitments may or may not give you an easy entrance point into this concept of commitment. The church is designed to fill in the gaps in our experience of an open nurturing family life.

- Explain a little about your experience of "family" in a church and whether your nuclear family life helped or hindered that experience.

[handwritten annotations: frustrated, disbelief, meh, joking, happy with corresponding emoji faces]

Now to get more specific. In Acts 2:42–47 we see how the people of the church in Jerusalem responded to the Good News of Jesus by building a church family. You'll find 4 commitments in verse 42.

- Make a list and describe details of how they would practice those commitments together.
- Discuss how your practice as a group family these next 8 weeks will mirror any of those commitments. What do you think will grow from those practices?
- How do you think the regular practice of any one of those commitments will shape you personally?
- Is there a fearful component to that prospect?
- Do you foresee any possible frustrations?
- Pray right now for each other's concerns.

We all experience the pros and cons of family life. Jesus' disciples exhibited something unique as a traveling band in the 1st Century, especially when you pick up the detail that there were a few women traveling with these thirteen men. The only way this would have been considered acceptable in the towns they visited would be evidence of interaction that would create the assumption of a family tie among the group. Open care and respect had to be evident and would have been accepted as proof of family connection in that extended family-driven culture. When you consider the assortment of people that made up this band of disciples this is clearly an example of how Jesus binds us together as family—not only in a way that is understood by us within the church, but also in a way that is visible to observers looking in on us.

- How will the development of a family relationship within your group be visible to people outside of your group?

Trinity's Family Values Box

Trinity's Family Values appear on page v. We'll be unpacking them throughout our *This Is Us* conversations, but go there now, read through them, and identify any Acts 2:42–47 connections and any connections to your conversation about your group family life.

CLOSING

Psalm 30
Responses adapted from Psalm 30 (CEV).

Leader: Heavenly Father, we learn from your Word that the early church gathered together and had everything in common. They were a family bound together by their shared faith in Christ Jesus.

Group: By his blood we are dressed up in joy.

Leader: We know, Lord, that all families experience moments of trial, where the bonds of family are tested.

Group: You have turned for us our mourning into dancing.

Leader: We pray then, Lord, that those tests would bind us together in a way that shows the world we are a family that has everything in common in you.

Group: By your favor, O Lord, you made us a strong mountain.

Leader: We pray that we will be able to gather together in this series to hear of your mighty works, your boundless love and your endless mercy.

Group: We sing praises to the Lord and give thanks to his holy name.

Leader: We pray for your guidance, O Lord, to those you would have join our family for this series.

Group: We will extol you, O Lord, because you have pulled us up.

Leader: And we seek your forgiveness whenever we don't live up to the title of brother or sister.

Group: Lord, listen and have mercy on us! O Lord, be our helper.

Leader: Lastly we pray that your Holy Spirit would lead this group. We pray all this in Jesus' name.

All: Amen.

WEEK 1 PRAYER NOTES PAGE

- Judy Schaeffer — kidney cancer
  wife of John S.
  communion server
- Jeanneen's mother in law Lucille — melanoma
- Patty's mom — knee replacement recovery
- Cheryl's co-workers; cancer treatment
  & niece, having a baby.

M. Trubinski & Bears
- peace in our world

TODAY'S TEXT

Just to make the idea of meditation and reflection a little more relevant, we've set up the exercise as a text stream, one for each of five days between your sessions. The first text is from Jesus himself... a message from the Word. You have the opportunity to react with an emoji. We've joined the stream with a comment and a question from our writing team. Lastly, you get to enter your prayer reply to Jesus. That may be an honest plea for help, a praise for newly discovered grace or purpose, a statement of commitment, or a plea for someone you know or for Trinity... or all of the above.

TODAY'S TEXT: WE ARE A GROWING FAMILY, DAY 1

JC: But the Holy Spirit will come upon you and give you power. Then you will tell everyone about me in Jerusalem, in all Judea, in Samaria, and everywhere in the world. (Acts 1:8 CEV)

(my reaction)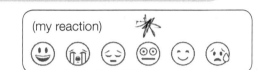

JP: The disciples are losing their leader a second time, this time to heaven for an unknown time. He's repeating the Great Commission to his disciples but it gets further away. Jerusalem ⇨ Judea ⇨ Samaria ⇨ to all. Like a raindrop ripple in a pond.

JP: What rippling journey has God taken me on as his representative?

(my prayer reply to JC)

going on work camp trips with more family & friends

TODAY'S TEXT: WE ARE A GROWING FAMILY, DAY 2

JC: But Jesus replied to the one who told Him, "Who is My mother and who are My brothers?" And stretching out His hand toward His disciples (and all His other followers), He said, "Here are My mother and My brothers! For whoever does the will of My Father who is in heaven by believing in Me, and following Me is My brother and sister and mother." (Matthew 12:48–49 AMP)

(my reaction)

JP: So many family meals shared. Even years later I can call the people who helped me become a Christ follower and it's just like talking to family: they can tell it to me straight, but truth always comes wrapped in love.
I feel like that's Jesus' tone here when he asks, "Who is my mother, and who are my brothers?" There's the kind of people who have just walked in, sheepishly late. "Good to see you."
And one day hopefully they "become" the people who go to all the trouble to get one person in the door. They know the truth and extend the love.

JP: Who's in the picture? Who in your Trinity church family would you title mother, father, brother, sister?

(my prayer reply to JC)

TODAY'S TEXT: WE ARE A GROWING FAMILY, DAY 3

> *JC: It was he who gave some to be apostles, some to be prophets, some to be evangelists, and some to be pastors and teachers, to prepare God's people for works of service, so that the body of Christ may be built up.* (Ephesians 4:11–12 NIV)

Good :)

(my reaction)

> JP: Feel like tweeting (or even being quotable) is beyond you, too? Be fair to yourself! God has gifted you also: you joyfully meet needs in ways that never occur to me. I'm oblivious. But I sure do love it when families serve together at church. It's wonderful to see kids (and parents) learning their God-gifting.

> JP: Which servants can you identify in the Trinity family?

(my prayer reply to JC)

Communion team
Readers
Pastors
praise band
choirs
Greeting team
Anyone!

TODAY'S TEXT: WE ARE A GROWING FAMILY, DAY 4

JC: God wants us to grow up, to know the whole truth and tell it in love—like Christ in everything. We take our lead from Christ, who is the source of everything we do. He keeps us in step with each other. His very breath and blood flow through us, nourishing us so that we will grow up healthy in God, robust in love.
(Ephesians 4:16 MSG)

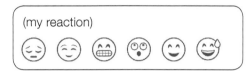
(my reaction)

JP: Verse 15 ends with Christlikeness. I wonder if that perfection keeps some people from using their abilities. Fear of mistakes? Verse 15: speaking truth in love, each of us grows up into Christ. Verse 16: from Christ ⇨, the whole church is joined together and grows up. Individuals ⇨ Christ ⇨ Church. Christ is the center.

JP: Grow up! Become robust! Yet, how can we hold each other up when mistakes happen? How can we encourage willingness to be sent… even when uncomfortable?

(my prayer reply to JC)
- time is inhibitor for me
- Learn from mistakes & go on
- it is all about grace!

TODAY'S TEXT: WE ARE A GROWING FAMILY, DAY 5

JC: God's various gifts are handed out everywhere; but they all originate in God's Spirit. God's various ministries are carried out everywhere; but they all originate in God's Spirit. God's various expressions of power are in action everywhere; but God himself is behind it all. (1 Corinthians 12:4–6 MSG)

(my reaction)

JP: So if Trinity is a big part of my spiritual family in Christ, and "the same God works all [gifts, service, and working] in all brothers and sisters," it makes me want to find out about how God is at work through the people of Trinity. I want to know more about different sites and teams.

JP: The Spirit decides who gets what, and when. Who can I ask, "What has the Spirit been doing with you? How can I pray for you?"

(my prayer reply to JC)

Maybe work more w/ high school youth + Shine

WEEK 2 – WE GO WHERE THE SPIRIT LEADS US

Acts 16:1–15

WORSHIP

Psalm 106

Today's psalm gives a long, yes a very long, account of how Israel was led by God, including the times they went their own way. This history is given to raise up praise in the community for God's faithfulness, not to commiserate about their failures. Read through Psalm 106 verse by verse at a very relaxed pace around the circle of your group giving each verse time to perc. A variety of translations is fine. At the end invite any individual(s) to give an account of a bump in the road they encountered this week and praise God for his faithfulness—already seen or still awaited.

VIDEO

Notes:

Trinity Family Values
Worship
Connect
Serve
Sharing

This family of God were ___led___ by the Holy Spirit.

They were led by being daily in ___prayer___, daily in ___God's Word___, and by doing it ___together___.

Are we open to ___discover___ the greater work God wants to do through us?

DISCUSSION

Read through Acts 16:1–15 together to get oriented.

"They" in verse 6 refers to Paul, Silas, and Timothy. As they follow Paul's intentions for this second missionary journey to travel east they run into closed doors.

- What do you think happened in 16:7? How do you think they experienced this barrier to their plans; sleepless nights, disagreements, hesitation and unease? How would it feel to you?

- Why would it be a good step to take these closed doors into prayer as a team? Describe several petitions you would have voiced if you had been on the team.

- Why would the team have discussed their goals and evaluated them in the light of God's Word?

- If you've ever felt the restraining hand of God, tell the group your story. What questions came to mind? How did you feel in that moment? What did you learn as a result?

- Can you recall a time Trinity hit a barrier? Do you know how goals were discussed and evaluated?

Acts 16: 8-10 Looking at the map tracking Paul's second missionary journey we can see that Paul's plan would have taken them north into new provinces of present day Turkey. Blocked, but without clear direction they continue along the road they are on to Troas, where they receive the call to Macedonia—Greece for a rather quick turn-around for Paul's plans. Guidance has now come not only circumstantially but also extraordinarily in vision. The team's discussion and prayers have become clear. They take ship passage west. If you trace their trail through Greece you bump into some very familiar names.

- With hindsight, we can celebrate what God has done in redirecting Paul's path. How eager are you to leave what seems good and discover the greater work God wants to do through you?

Paul's Missionary Journeys   ©Concordia Publishing House

- How can we hear the Spirit, especially when he says, "not that way, but this way"? (Consider not only the extraordinary vision, but the ordinary of circumstance.)

- How can we know the Spirit well enough, both as a church and as individual believers, to trust him when he leads us into something bigger—and harder? (Notice the guidance comes after they've already taken their first steps on the journey.)

- What in Trinity's current plans requires trust?

Colossians 4:2–6 (NLT)

> ²Devote yourselves to prayer with an alert mind and a thankful heart. ³Pray for us, too, that God will give us many opportunities to speak about his mysterious plan concerning Christ. That is why I am here in chains. ⁴Pray that I will proclaim this message as clearly as I should. ⁵Live wisely among those who are not believers, and make the most of every opportunity. ⁶Let your conversation be gracious and attractive so that you will have the right response for everyone.

- How might Paul's experiences from Acts 16:1–15 shaped his attitude in this text? What does this teach us about listening to God's Spirit in prayer? *you might not always hear what you expected*
- *trust* — How can we know the Spirit well enough, both as a church and as individual believers, to trust him when he leads us into something bigger—and harder?

- How might this change your own prayer life and how you schedule your days as a result?

- Use Colossians 4:2–6 to build some prayer points for finding God's direction to an opportunity to further his kingdom. Pray that prayer together right now.

The request received in the vision (Acts 16:9) convey an earnestness, soliciting an emotionally driven response. Romans 5:8 (GW) *Christ died for us while we were still sinners. This demonstrates God's love for us* indicates Jesus' desire for us, his willingness to take action despite our condition or status.

- If God cares that much for us, how much do you care for the people he will lead across your path tomorrow? If you consider a range of attitudes, which would you admit to when asked to venture out of your comfort zone towards God's opportunity?

Acts 16:11–15   We see Paul keeping the appointment God had already set up for him. Paul's willingness to change plans was a huge blessing to Philippi. How do you follow God's lead? Here are a few suggestions. Consider them and add your own to the list.

- Examine your spheres of influence (family, neighborhood, workplace) for someone far from God, a possible relationship you could take to a new level. Begin with prayer. We recommend that everyone in your group have a **Two Plus** heading in your prayer list containing the names of at least two people who don't know Jesus. Discuss the possible names for your **Two Plus** list with your group seeking prayer and guidance. Is God nudging you to invite them to next week's session?

- Get into the habit of having **Level 1 Contacts**—simply saying "Hi" to someone you don't know and introducing yourself. It is a basic kind of intro discussion with someone you just happen to meet in line at the grocery, someone regularly in your train car, or another parent at the park.

- Watch for the opportunity to move to **Level 2 Contacts.** Take the next step in the relationship by inviting them and their spouse for dinner, to catch a movie, or meeting for coffee—being intentional in furthering the relationship. This will require you to shift your time use, your priorities to include space to *Be with Somebody.* It's hard to be authentic in a newly developing relationship if you're always in a rush.

- Watch for a fork in the road of conversation. Listen with your heart for open doors to talk about God's love and forgiveness.

- Be a resource provider. Your opportunity may not be to deliver a sermon, but to point someone toward a resource; a book you've read, a podcast, a song, a small group event or coming sermon series. Or it might be offering tools and a little help for a home project.

CLOSING

Psalm 106

Responses adapted from Psalm 106 (CEV).

Leader: Heavenly Father, we seek to do your will, and often we strike out on our own,
Group: Hoping that you will bless our efforts.

Leader: But as the nation of Israel learned, you had your own plan for them and their future.
Group: Paul, Silas and Timothy trusted your words; let us trust your words too.

Leader: So, we steadfastly pray, Lord, that the doors you have for us would open, and that we would hear when your Holy Spirit says "no" to our direction.
Group: We seek your wisdom so we can experience the good things your chosen ones experienced.

Leader: Your saving the world was accomplished through this plan.
Group: So we rejoice in joy as your nation.

Leader: And we know, Lord, that your desire to reach the whole world will be accomplished through your church.
Group: So we praise you because we belong to you.

Leader: We pray for the will to act, just as our brother Jesus acted on our behalf.
Group: So we can give thanks to your holy name and rejoice in your praise!

Leader: Let all the people say:
All: Amen. Praise the Lord!

WEEK 2 PRAYER NOTES PAGE

TWO **PLUS**

TODAY'S TEXT: WE GO WHERE THE SPIRIT LEADS US, DAY 1

JC: For all who are led by the Spirit of God are children of God. (Romans 8:14 NLT)

(my reaction)

GP: Paul and Philip had plans, goals, and dreams. Yet when the Spirit called, Philip was led to a man on a road; Paul to Europe. The Spirit led them; they listened to their Father's voice and changed the world. Time and the urgent control my life. I try to control time, but it controls me. Holy Spirit, help me hear you!

GP: What is one thing that is blocking you from being led by the Spirit?

(my prayer reply to JC)

TODAY'S TEXT: WE GO WHERE THE SPIRIT LEADS US, DAY 2

JC: Now listen, you who say, "Today or tomorrow we will go to this or that city, spend a year there, carry on business and make money." Why, you do not even know what will happen tomorrow. What is your life? You are a mist that appears for a little while and then vanishes. Instead, you ought to say, "If it is the Lord's will, we will live and do this or that." (James 4:13–15 NIV)

(my reaction)

GP: We create schedules, day planners, 1-year plans, 5-year plans. We do this individually and as a church. But, it all comes to nothing if we don't ask God what he wants us to do, where he wants us to go. We know we have a mission to help others know you Jesus, help us to see the doors you have opened and the doors you have closed.

GP: What is an area of your life in which you need to turn over control to God?

(my prayer reply to JC)

TODAY'S TEXT: WE GO WHERE THE SPIRIT LEADS US, DAY 3

JC: And when they bring you before the synagogues and the rulers and the authorities, do not be anxious about how you should defend yourself or what you should say, for the Holy Spirit will teach you in that very hour what you ought to say.
(Luke 12:11–12 ESV)

(my reaction) 😍 😎 😐 😫

GP: If I'm to rely on your Spirit, I guess I need to be in the Word and prayer daily. It's hard to rely on someone when you never talk to them or listen to them. I get it. I continually need to seek direction and guidance for both Trinity and my life.

GP: What's the issue for you, finding the time or being regular when it comes to your communication with God? What one thing could you do to address that?

(my prayer reply to JC)

TODAY'S TEXT: WE GO WHERE THE SPIRIT LEADS US, DAY 4

JC: When the Spirit of truth comes, he will guide you into all truth. He will not speak on his own but will tell you what he has heard. He will tell you about the future. (John 16:13 NLT)

(my reaction)

GP: So the Spirit is going to guide me. He's going to accompany me, be right by my side, helping me to understand God's truth for my life and for the life of Trinity. The more I understand where he's guiding me, the better I'll know where I'm headed now and in the future. How cool is that!

GP: How has the Spirit guided you in the past? How can you use this knowledge to help guide you in a decision you need to make now?

(my prayer reply to JC)

TODAY'S TEXT: WE GO WHERE THE SPIRIT LEADS US, DAY 5

JC: Do not be conformed to this world, but be transformed by the renewal of your mind, that by testing you may discern what is the will of God, what is good and acceptable and perfect.
(Romans 12:2 ESV)

(my reaction)

GP: It's hard to stick out, to not conform. Everything the world tells me is contrary to what God tells me. I want to follow God's will. I want to be led by the Spirit. I don't want to do it alone. I can't do it alone! I need my church family to support and encourage me.

GP: Who helps you hear and follow the Spirit?

(my prayer reply to JC)

WEEK 3 GOD DOES AMAZING THINGS THROUGH US

Acts 19:1–20

WORSHIP

Jesus is declared King of Kings and Lord of Lords by his resurrection. Read the psalm together celebrating Jesus our King. Pause before closing with verse 13 to let individuals bring a praise for evidence of God's hand seen this week.

Psalm 21:1–8, 13 (GW)

[1] *The king finds joy in your strength, O L*ORD*.*
    What great joy he has in your victory!

[2] *You gave him his heart's desire.*
    You did not refuse the prayer from his lips.   Selah

[3] *You welcomed him with the blessings of good things*
    and set a crown of fine
    gold on his head.

[4] *He asked you for life.*
    You gave him a long life, forever and ever.

[5] *Because of your victory his glory is great.*
    You place splendor and majesty on him.

[6] *Yes, you made him a blessing forever.*
    You made him glad with the joy of your presence.

[7] *Indeed, the king trusts the L*ORD*,*
    and through the mercy of
    the Most High, he will not
    be moved.

[8] *Your hand will discover*
    all your enemies.
    Your powerful hand will
    find all who hate you.

    (pause)

Trinity Family Values

Worship
Serve
Sharing
Accountability

[13] *Arise, O L*ORD*, in your strength.*
    We will sing and make music to praise your power.

VIDEO

Read Acts 19:1–20 individually to get oriented before you watch the video. You may want to refer again to the map of Paul's Journeys on page 19. Mark any verse, word or phrase that catches your attention or causes a question, but save it for later—no discussion now, then watch the video.

Notes:

God takes __ordinary__ people and uses them in __extraordinary__ ways.

Sometimes we seek to get our __prayers answered__ by striking a deal with God.

God will use the supernatural power of his __Spirit__ for his __mission__.

His primary goal is to align our __hearts__ with his.

DISCUSSION

Acts 19:1-8 Paul arrives in Ephesus and wastes no time in establishing a core group of 12 believers. Note how the Holy Spirit empowers them for the spread of the Gospel.

- What gifts of the Holy Spirit have you seen in action at Trinity? See the gifts listed in these texts for a kick start: Romans 12:4–8, 1 Corinthians 12:4–11, 27–28.

Paul then, as is often his custom, goes to the local synagogue to present the Good News of Jesus to the Jewish community who would be primed to hear of God's Messiah.

- What adjectives are given in your translation for the reception Paul received in the synagogue?

- Why would they disparage Paul's message about the Kingdom of God which includes all people in contrast to a Jewish Kingdom over all people?
- How would an exclusionary or self-serving orientation at Trinity hobble our ministry? *would not keep expanding as Trinity has*
- Why would Paul continue in the face of opposition at the synagogue for three months?

Acts 19:9 & 10 Paul's next step is to set up another base location for daily preaching where he would be free to interact with Gentiles as well as Jews using what would have been the "siesta" hour. Paul supported himself and his team during his journeys. You can see another example of this in Acts 18:1–4. His trade as a tent maker would have been conducted in the market place during normal shop hours. But, during the customary midday break, Paul continues to labor under his calling to bring people to Christ. He labors from the fall of approximately 52AD to 55AD. In those few years the Ephesus church becomes not just a congregation but a hub for the whole region. Do I hear anyone say multi-site? 😄

- Where do you think Paul was having **Level 1** contacts? *tent maker & vendor*
- How would he have entered **Level 2?** *bringing people to meeting site*
- How are you using your siesta time?
- Where could you get the energy to follow Paul's kind of schedule? *asking for courage & strength*

Acts 19:11, 12 In Acts 19:6f we saw the Holy Spirit invest Paul's core team with power. Now we see another "power advance" in the mission. (For other examples in Acts check out 5:16, 8:7, 16:16–18) 😳 Besides tents and awnings, Paul would have worked a variety of canvas and leather items. "Handkerchiefs"—perhaps sweatbands, aprons or belts that were in contact with or made by Paul, were carried away from Paul's shop and apparently having amazing impact, like the story of Peter's shadow in Acts 5:15. The healings connected to the items were an advance affirmation of the Spirit's power in Paul's ministry and the truth of his words. The action of the Holy Spirit in Paul's ministry was enticing, attractive to the population.

- What in your experience would you label as an act of God?
- What in Trinity's ministry do you think draws attention to the power of God?

Acts 19:13-20 Josephus, a Jewish historian, tells us that Jews scattered in the Roman world often served as mediators or bridges between the magical wisdom of the East and the Western Greco-Roman concrete mindset. They would often operate as exorcists. And so, we meet the Sons of Sceva. The claim of descent from a High Priest would be credentials among the Gentile population for direct access to the divine. The formula would be to pile name upon powerful name to create an incantation powerful enough to require a spirit to do one's bidding. The backfire in this story is proof of the supremacy of the Holy Spirit moving in the ministry of Paul.

- Is it reasonable to expect the Holy Spirit to work in unexpected or amazing ways today? Why or why not and in what context?
- Jesus supplies everything including power that we need to carry out the mission he has given us. Would you describe your life as a disciple as powerful or tapped out? Explain
- What do you think was the key in Paul's role as a conduit of the power of the Holy Spirit? (Consider constancy in God's Word, regular prayer, a disciplined and generous heart.) How do you think those disciplines would serve your life in the Spirit?

When writing to the congregation in Corinth, Paul closes his discussion of the great variety and function of spiritual gifts in chapter 12 with these words: *Are we all apostles? Are we all prophets? Are we all teachers? Do we all have the power to do miracles? Do we all have the gift of healing? Do we all have the ability to speak in unknown languages? Do we all have the ability to interpret unknown languages? Of course not! So you should earnestly desire the most helpful gifts. But now let me show you a way of life that is best of all. If I could speak all the languages of earth and of angels, but didn't love others, I would only be a noisy gong or a clanging cymbal. If I had the gift of prophecy, and if I understood all of God's secret plans and possessed all knowledge, and if I had such faith that I could* move mountains, but didn't love others, I would be nothing. If I gave everything I have to the poor and even sacrificed my body, I could boast about it; but if I didn't love others, I would have gained nothing. Love is patient and kind. Love is not jealous or boastful or proud or rude. It does not demand its own way. It is not irritable, and it keeps no record of being wronged. It does not rejoice about injustice but rejoices whenever the truth wins out. Love never gives up, never loses faith, is always hopeful, and endures through every circumstance. 1 Corinthians 12:29–13:7 (NLT)

- How can your spiritual gifts be used with love to point to Jesus and his love and grace? Use your group's discussion to formulate prayer points for the prayer notes page. *serving others*
- Add "Ask the Holy Spirit to fill our hearts to "earnestly desire" the helpful function of our giftedness through his power."

CLOSING

Psalm 21
Responses adapted from Psalm 21 (CEV).

Leader: Heavenly father, you're bold Word created the universe.
Group: And we celebrate your strength Lord.

Leader: By the blood of your son Jesus, your Word declares that we are forgiven.
Group: And look how happy we are about your saving help!

Leader: You have restored us to a relationship with you that we may ask anything in the Son's name.
Group: And you haven't denied what our lips requested.

Leader: But too often Lord, we pray for things that are not aligned to your will.
Group: We devised a wicked plan—but we did fail!

Leader: Or we have not trusted the power in your Spirit to accomplish what we desire; so we remain silent.
Group: But you would give us what our heart desires.

Leader: So today Lord we pray boldly in the power of your Holy Spirit. We pray knowing that through Jesus, your ear hears the requests of our hearts. We pray for…

(list each prayer petition one at a time, the group responds to each with the following):

Group: Be exalted, Lord, in your strength! We will sing and praise your power!

Leader: We pray for these rich blessings right to us in the name of your son Jesus whose Word gives us life.

Group: You put a crown of pure gold on our heads.

All: Amen.

WEEK 3 PRAYER NOTES PAGE

Carol, Chip's colleague
use GroupMe more

TWO **PLUS**

TODAY'S TEXT: GOD DOES AMAZING THINGS THROUGH US, DAY 1

JC: This miraculous sign at Cana in Galilee was the first time Jesus revealed his glory. And his disciples believed in him.
(John 2:11 NLT)

(my reaction)

MF: Even behind the scenes, Jesus, your actions are designed to impact lives and bring faith. What purpose you pour into every action! They came to celebrate a wedding and ended up celebrating you.

MF: How has God worked behind the scenes of your life?

(my prayer reply to JC)

TODAY'S TEXT: GOD DOES AMAZING THINGS THROUGH US, DAY 2

JC: I tell you the truth, anyone who believes in me will do the same works I have done, and even greater works, because I am going to be with the Father. (John 14:12 NLT)

MF: Jesus, you've really set me up with this one. I want to jump into my day knowing you have a great plan for it, but I don't want to be opportunistic like those sons of Sceva. I also feel a little swamped by the God-sized impact you describe!

MF: What God-sized impact do you see needed in your day?

(my prayer reply to JC)

TODAY'S TEXT: GOD DOES AMAZING THINGS THROUGH US, DAY 3

JC: God's Spirit makes us sure that we are his children.
(Romans 8:16 CEV)

(my reaction)

MF: I see! It's all about your love and grace, Jesus, not about me! Love and grace that extends far beyond me, yet through me. I don't have to be Paul, I can be faithfully me. I'm waiting to follow your cue.

MF: Who could use a glimpse of your confidence in God today?

(my prayer reply to JC)

TODAY'S TEXT: GOD DOES AMAZING THINGS THROUGH US, DAY 4

JC: In fact, all I will talk about is how Christ let me speak and work, so that the Gentiles would obey him, Indeed, I will tell how Christ worked miracles and wonders by the power of the Holy Spirit. (Romans 15:18–19a CEV)

(my reaction)

MF: Ooooo, Paul had a plan to talk about Jesus' presence and action in his own life. The focus stays on him and what happens is powered by the Holy Spirit. Jesus' signs and wonders are happening all around me. I notice and report.

MF: So what is the story of Jesus' wonders in your life?

(my prayer reply to JC)

TODAY'S TEXT: GOD DOES AMAZING THINGS THROUGH US, DAY 5

JC: The signs of a true apostle were performed among you with utmost patience, with signs and wonders and mighty works.
(2 Corinthians 12:12 ESV)

(my reaction)

MF: Hmmm, Paul set the model for the Corinthian believers in relying on God to back up his words about Jesus with amazing confirmation. Now he's calling them out to live out a wonder-filled faith, too.

Who sets the model for you? Who calls confidently on God's help and will guide you in that confidence? Who challenges you to live the model you've seen?

(my prayer reply to JC)

WEEK 4 WE TAKE RISKS FOR THE GOSPEL

Acts 6:8–7:60

WORSHIP

Read Psalm 116 together out loud, one section at a time with a pause for reflection between each. When you have come to the end of the psalm, complete your promise to God of thanksgiving by telling the group about when God listened to you and showed his faithfulness.

Psalm 116 (MSG)

> $^{1-6}$ *I love God because he listened to me,*
> *listened as I begged for mercy.*
>
> *He listened so intently*
> *as I laid out my case before him.*
>
> *Death stared me in the face,*
> *hell was hard on my heels.*
>
> *Up against it, I didn't know which way to turn;*
> *then I called out to God for help:*
>
> *"Please, God!" I cried out.*
> *"Save my life!"*
>
> *God is gracious—it is he who makes things right,*
> *our most compassionate God.*
>
> *God takes the side of the helpless;*
> *when I was at the end of my rope, he saved me.*

> $^{7-8}$ *I said to myself, "Relax and rest.*
> *God has showered you with blessings.*
> *Soul, you've been rescued from death;*
> *Eye, you've been rescued from tears;*
> *And you, Foot, were kept from stumbling."*

---

⁹⁻¹¹ I'm striding in the presence of God,
  alive in the land of the living!
I stayed faithful, though bedeviled,
  and despite a ton of bad luck,
Despite giving up on the human race,
  saying, "They're all liars and cheats."

———————

¹²⁻¹⁹ What can I give back to God
  for the blessings he's poured out on me?
I'll lift high the cup of salvation—a toast to God!
  I'll pray in the name of God;
I'll complete what I promised God I'd do,
  and I'll do it together with his people.
When they arrive at the gates of death,
  God welcomes those who love him.
Oh, God, here I am, your servant,
  your faithful servant: set me free for your service!
I'm ready to offer the thanksgiving sacrifice
  and pray in the name of God.
I'll complete what I promised God I'd do,
  and I'll do it in company with his people,
In the place of worship, in God's house,
  in Jerusalem, God's city.
  Hallelujah!

VIDEO

Notes:

Know the Good News of

Jesus Christ will cause

_____.

Trinity Family Values

Leading
Sharing
Accountability

Know that following Jesus means I must be _____.

Know that you are not _____; this is US, not this is YOU.

Acts 6:8–7:60
Read the whole story dividing it up in sections but without pausing for comment. Circle one or more emoji as you read.

We first meet Stephen (Acts 6:1–7) in the listing of newly appointed deacons charged with the care ministry for widows, but in tonight's text we see him taking a step into preaching/teaching/evangelizing even in the face of opposition. He has followed God's nudge into another area. Why shouldn't we be surprised by a risk factor in following God's nudge? (This is an onion, peel off all the layers.)

Remember Stephen was part of a team of deacons. What kind of script would you write for Stephen's meeting with his team the day or two before his sermon? Take some time to discuss this. Include an element of decision making about Stephen's nudge to speak and the nature of the group's support for his decision.

What do you hear in Stephen's sermon that would give him the confidence to preach it?

Share a threat point, subtle or tangible, that you have experienced around your witness or faithfulness to Jesus, perhaps among your extended family, neighborhood, or workplace.

- How does your faith divide you or mark you in that setting?
- Why does the possibility of a negative response cause you to withdraw?
- Why is authenticity difficult?
- Why is authenticity essential?

In the video, Pastor Dave references Matthew 28:18–20. Read it together. Notice that this passage, often called the Great Commission, begins with Jesus' authority and ends with the promise of his presence. How does Jesus' authority and presence encourage you in your own witness?

The key elements we hear in all the sermons in Acts is the good news of Jesus' death and resurrection; the saving action of God that brings us all redemption and the proof of God's eternal intention for us that gives us hope. What could you say about redemption and hope to one person in that family, neighborhood, or workplace situation—perhaps the person you've been praying for?

- What kind of risk support would you like from the group to move this conversation from the hypothetical to reality?
- Ways to Prepare and Practice on Your Own:
  - This is probably a person you've established a **Level 1** connection with—a "Hi" regular greeting kind of relationship, and moved on to **Level 2**—developing that casual recognition into a relationship with shared experience such as invitations to the house, shared recreational or social activities, personal conversations.
  - Review what you know about this person, their dreams and their heartaches. Find a path of approach.
  - Write a personal brief "then/now" account of your life with Jesus—the impact he has on your dreams and heartaches. This doesn't have to be a dramatic conversion story. We all have made bad choices at some time and feel the joy of a new beginning through God's grace.
  - Practice with someone from your small group for encouragement and to check that it "hears" the way you intend.
  - Tell your group of your plans so they can check on your progress.

CLOSING

Responses adapted from Psalm 116 (CEV).

Leader: Dearest Lord, we live in a world hostile to your truth. We call out to you as long as we live

Group: Because you listen closely to us.

Leader: You have charged your followers to be your witnesses to the ends of the earth. But we see the risk of speaking on your behalf and hesitate.

Group: You, God, have delivered us from death, my eyes from tears, and our feet from stumbling.

Leader: So we'll walk before the Lord in the land of the living. If you are for us, what can man do to us?

Group: We tell ourselves, we can be at peace again, because the Lord has been good to you.

Leader: Lord be faithful to us when we hesitate, when we say "I am suffering so badly."

Group: Even when I say out of fear "Everyone is a liar"

Leader: Lord, give us confidence in the face of persecution, even the persecution of death.

Group: What can we give back to the Lord for all the good things he has done for us?

Leader: Lord give us the confidence to take risks for the Gospel.

Group: To risk all to bring the good news to the lost.

Leader: We call on the Lord's name:

All: Lord, please save us. Amen.

WEEK 4 PRAYER NOTES PAGE

TWO **PLUS**

TODAY'S TEXT: WE TAKE RISKS FOR THE GOSPEL, DAY 1

JC: Anyone who wants to live all out for Christ is in for a lot of trouble; there's no getting around it. Unscrupulous con men will continue to exploit the faith. (2 Timothy 3:12 MSG)

(my reaction)

JP: Jesus has paid the price for me! No suffering to earn anything.
But if he suffered, surely I will as his follower. Being all in for Jesus brings its own unavoidable trouble.
Paradox: to gain life, lose life. This isn't the "God wants to bless you" prosperity message of TV evangelists.

JP: What danger and challenges surround our Trinity family?

(my prayer reply to JC)

TODAY'S TEXT: WE TAKE RISKS FOR THE GOSPEL, DAY 2

JC: The signs of a true apostle were performed among you with utmost patience, with signs and wonders and mighty works.
(2 Corinthians 12:12 ESV)

(my reaction)

JP: Don't take it personally—seems easy to write. We do it all the time, assigning personal involvement to those who follow… wearing a sports team t-shirt, or listening to a band's music. Followers do represent the leader.

JP: Where does flak and fault assigning start when you lead and follow at Trinity?

(my prayer reply to JC)

TODAY'S TEXT: WE TAKE RISKS FOR THE GOSPEL, DAY 3

JC: Happy are those who are persecuted because they do what God requires; the Kingdom of heaven belongs to them!
(Matthew 5:10 GNB)

(my reaction)

JP: Life continues on the road of enduring maligning. God requirements loom large. So does the ransom and reward. The end reward is heaven.

JP: If mistreatment is to be expected, the question becomes "How do I continue in what I've learned in the Bible?" even when the going is hardest. How do I stay on the road and not cry, "Uncle"?

(my prayer reply to JC)

TODAY'S TEXT: WE TAKE RISKS FOR THE GOSPEL, DAY 4

JC: Yes, we live under constant danger of death because we serve Jesus, so that the life of Jesus will be evident in our dying bodies. (2 Corinthians 4:11 NLT)

(my reaction)

JP: End of the rope isn't the end of hope. The weakest me becomes an expansive opportunity for God's power to pick up the fragments. Daily living in Christ is dangerous. And it's truly living.

JP: He won't fail you, so how can you think sharing the Gospel all rests on you? Couldn't the story he's writing be like a mosaic of us all, viewed from his perspective?

(my prayer reply to JC)

TODAY'S TEXT: WE TAKE RISKS FOR THE GOSPEL, DAY 5

JC: I kept my bearings in Christ—but I entered their world and tried to experience things from their point of view. I've become just about every sort of servant there is in my attempts to lead those I meet into a God-saved life. (1 Corinthians 9:22 MSG)

(my reaction)

JP: "Fake it till you make it" doesn't always go down well. Neither does swooping into a situation to be a "savior." Try Paul's approach: You live here? In the neighborhood? Let me show you around. Hardly anyone who doesn't yet know Jesus has ever refused my offer to pray right there in response to a concern.

JP: Can you, who are so different, start with finding common ground with _____? Can you start by listening to _____'s hurts and needs?

(my prayer reply to JC)

WEEK 5   SOMETIMES WE DON'T GET ALONG
Acts 15:36–41

WORSHIP

When your boat starts rocking on the seas of life, it's always good to remember who is the Master. Read this psalm together praising God, then let each recall an instance of stability God brought about this week and give the glory to him.

Psalm 46 (ESV)

¹ God is our refuge and strength,
   a very present help in trouble.
² Therefore we will not fear though the earth gives way,
   though the mountains be moved into the heart of the sea,
³ though its waters roar and foam,
   though the mountains tremble at its swelling.   Selah
⁴ There is a river whose streams make glad the city of God,
   the holy habitation of the Most High.   *Holy Spirit*
⁵ God is in the midst of her; she shall not be moved;
   God will help her when morning dawns.
⁶ The nations rage, the kingdoms totter;
   he utters his voice, the earth melts.
⁷ The Lord of hosts is with us;
   the God of Jacob is our fortress.   Selah
⁸ Come, behold the works of the Lord,
   how he has brought desolations on the earth.
⁹ He makes wars cease to the end of the earth;
   he breaks the bow and shatters the spear;
   he burns the chariots with fire.
¹⁰ "Be still, and know that I am God.
   I will be exalted among the nations,
   I will be exalted in the earth!"
¹¹ The Lord of hosts is with us;
   the God of Jacob is our fortress.   Selah

VIDEO

Notes:

When two or more people interact for a long enough time, _conflict happens_.

Trinity Family Values
Serve
Leading
Accountability

Is it possible that the disagreement, which brought about a split, was a _good_ thing, the _best_ outcome?

DISCUSSION

Start with this review of Paul and Barnabas' history together and describe the relationship you would expect to develop through their experiences together.

- Acts 2:26, 27 Barnabas, whose name means encourager, took the newly converted Saul/Paul under his wing when he first returned to Jerusalem. _they were friends_
- Acts 11:19-26 When a ministry was rising among Gentiles in Antioch, Barnabas was sent by church leaders in Jerusalem to work there as a church planter. Barnabas tracks down Saul/Paul inviting him to join in this ministry.
- Acts 11:27-30 The church in Antioch sends famine relief funds to Jerusalem in the care of Barnabas and Saul. (John Mark returns from Jerusalem with them.) _faith, trust by following_
- Acts 13:1-3 Saul and Barnabas are sent on mission by the church in Antioch. The account of this first missionary journey continues through Acts 14.
- ✗ Acts 15:1-19 (Sunday's sermon text) The Council at Jerusalem was a key moment in the journey of the early church and, as we heard in our Week 5 sermon, it was a decision forced by

disagreement. Notice that Paul and Barnabas are in the middle of the controversy because of their mission to Gentiles. It was a controversy well handled, a decision formed by recognizing the hand of God in the ministry and the blessing of the outcomes. Most importantly, we see the church affirm the primary point of grace through faith in Jesus (15:11). Paul and Barnabas happily return to their home base in Antioch with a well-reasoned, Spirit led decision from the leaders in Jerusalem. You feel a swell of anticipation for what will come next for Paul and Barnabas. 😃

Read Acts 15:36–41. Paul and Barnabas disagree about their next step in mission, particularly about the inclusion of John Mark (side bar) in the team. The translated phrase "sharp disagreement" 😠 in Greek is the same word used when Paul is "provoked" by Athens, a city full of idols. With few details here in the text, we sense not only the division over Mark's participation on the team, but the underlying issue of goal, where the team is next to pursue the mission. Paul wants to check-in on the churches they had planted on the later itinerary of their first journey.

- Consider together whether this may have a been a "division" of the team or a "birthing" of two teams. Let individuals in your group take the perspective of Paul and others take the perspective of Barnabas to debate. Give each group a few minutes to consolidate their perspective then begin the debate/discussion. Afterwards debrief:
  - How did it feel preparing your case? What was the challenge?
  - What were the most influential points made by the other group?
  - How did this activity strengthen of shift your take on this story?
- Do you think this was a private disagreement or might it have spilled over into the church in Antioch? Would that be good or bad?

The people involved in a disagreement each have a unique perspective. The difficulty is gaining an understanding of the other's perspective. One perspective may not be more right or more wrong. They each may have value. Often that understanding does not come immediately, but over time. We have lengthy hindsight and can see some of the outcomes from this split and companion choice by Barnabas and Paul. We can trace what God does in these lives, his faithfulness despite the turmoil. See what comes further down the road for some of the people affected by Paul and Barnabas' decision.

Acts 12:12 John, whose other name was Mark, assisted in the partnership of Paul and Barnabas (his cousin; Col 4:10) on the first part of their first missionary journey while they were on the island of Cyprus. Then we see a simple note that he returns to Jerusalem while Paul and Barnabas sail on for Perga (Turkey) (see v. 25; 13:5, 13). Why? One suggestion is homesickness, a young man unused to travel. Some scholars suggest a larger issue. Mark departs at the point where the mission begins to interact with Gentiles. Mark regained Paul's favor later (see Col. 4:10; 2 Tim. 4:11; Philem. 24) and accompanied Peter (see 1 Pet. 5:13). There is substantial testimony from the early church that he wrote the Gospel of Mark.

- Mark carries on an important assistant role (the spiritual gift of helps?) with Barnabas, Paul, and Peter. Possibly through his association with Peter he writes the Gospel of Mark.
- Paul's partnership with Silas was advantageous because both were Roman citizens (Acts 16:37) with equal ability to travel and work in any of the empire hub cities.
- Paul recruits Timothy (Acts 16:1–3) who is mentored into the next generation of church ministry.
- Paul has freedom to be responsive, change agenda and take the Gospel into Greece. Remember our Week 2 session on Acts 16:1–15? In verse 11 the pronoun "we" appears for Paul's team indicating Luke, the author of Acts and the Gospel of Luke, has joined Paul's troupe.

Turn your attention to "Conflicts Past," either personal or involving Trinity ministry team decisions. This is a family discussion, so do not enter into the life of other congregations or agencies. Be respectful of all who were involved. Be sensitive to members of the group who may have not shared your experience. Remember old wounds are healed by giving forgiveness. Reinforce the confidentiality of your group life.

- Were you involved personally… as a leader?
- Was there a process in place to bring about a resolution, including prayer?
- Was the process for understanding based on respect for each party's perspective?
- Was there a consideration of the long-term goal?
- Can you trace a long-term outcome from this conflict? Do you think God brought blessing into his kingdom through the conflict, or despite the conflict?

We shouldn't shy away from conflict when it arises in our church, our small groups, or in our ministry partnerships. It can be a symptom of growth and expansion of the ministry. However, we must be careful not to let it disable our ability to spread the Good News. Your personal history in church conflict can become a root of fear hampering your free response to the movement of the Holy Spirit. Our handling of conflict can tarnish the outside community's perspective of the church as followers of Jesus.

- Which of those points is a tender spot for you?
- Pray right now for the ministry of Trinity as we expand into a congregation with four sites and our proper handling of conflict. Commit to making this a regular part of your prayers for Trinity.

CLOSING

Before you begin, divide into A and B groups and assign a Leader voice.

Responses adapted from Psalm 46 (CEV).

    Leader: Heavenly Father, you are our creator. Your son Jesus has

	redeemed us by his blood. Your Holy Spirit has taught us the faith.
Group A:	**God is our refuge and strength,**
Group B:	**a help always near in times of great trouble.**
Leader:	But while we find our identity, our common purpose in you, we confess to you that we don't always get along with our brothers and sisters in faith.
Group A:	**God is in our city. It will never crumble.**
Group B:	**God will help us when morning dawns.**
Leader:	But you have created us to be unique individuals, breaking the mold with each of us,
Group A:	**The Lord of heavenly forces is with us!**
Group B:	**The God of Jacob is our place of safety.**
Leader:	We desire, Lord, that when conflict arises, we would remain cooperative. That both positions and all outcomes would seek to advance the Gospel.
Group A:	**God says: "That's enough! Now know that I am God!"**
Group B:	**"I am exalted among all nations; I am exalted throughout the world!"**
Leader:	We desire to remember that people in both sides of our conflicts,
Group A:	**…are your beloved children.**
Group B:	**…and are redeemed in Christ.**
Leader:	So we pray that our conflicts would be chances to further your Gospel and not hinder it.
Group A:	**God is our refuge and strength,**
Group B:	**a help always near in times of great trouble.**
Leader:	We pray this in the name of the one who unifies us in reconciliation to you.
All:	**We pray this in the name of our brother Christ. Amen.**

WEEK 5 PRAYER NOTES PAGE

Brian's brother - heart health & life issues
Patty's mom - rehab
Tina

TWO **PLUS**

TODAY'S TEXT: SOMETIMES WE DON'T GET ALONG, DAY 1

JC: Be at peace with one another. (Mark 9:50 ESV)

(my reaction)

MS: Easier said than done, Jesus. People disagree with me. They don't do what I think they should do. They have their own agenda. If I'm going to be at peace with others, I'm going to need your help. I'm going to need peace that "passes all understanding" that can only come from you.

MS: With whom do you need to share God's peace today?

(my prayer reply to JC)

TODAY'S TEXT: SOMETIMES WE DON'T GET ALONG, DAY 2

JC: I entreat Euodia and I entreat Syntyche to agree in the Lord. Yes, I ask you also, true companion, help these women, who have labored side by side with me in the gospel. (Philippians 4:2–3 ESV)

(my reaction)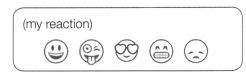

MS: I get it, Jesus. Getting along is a lot easier if we remember we are working together for the same cause. Sports teams all seem to have "great team chemistry" when they are winning. It's losing teams that have a hard time getting along. Maybe a lot of the problems we see with relationships in churches would go away if we just remembered we are on the winning team!

MS: Who are your "teammates" in sharing the Gospel these days?

(my prayer reply to JC)

TODAY'S TEXT: SOMETIMES WE DON'T GET ALONG, DAY 3

JC: Bear with one another in love. (Ephesians 4:2 ESV)

(my reaction)

MS: Love really is what it's all about, isn't it? You are a God of love, you call us to love one another, and that love becomes the witness to the world. If we try to "bear with one another" out of obedience or emotion, we will fail. But if we let our love for YOU, Jesus, shape how we feel about others, that will be the key!

MS: Who is hard for you to love right now?

(my prayer reply to JC)

TODAY'S TEXT: SOMETIMES WE DON'T GET ALONG, DAY 4

JC: Keep loving one another earnestly, since love covers a multitude of sins. (1 Peter 4:8 ESV)

(my reaction)

MS: Sometimes it is really important to confront sin in someone. They need my help dealing with an issue in their life. But there are times when forgiving and forgetting is best. Sometimes I need to let love cover the sin of someone around me. Jesus, please help me know when a sin needs to be confronted, or needs to be forgiven and forgotten.

MS: Is there something someone has done to you that you need to let love cover today?

(my prayer reply to JC)

TODAY'S TEXT: SOMETIMES WE DON'T GET ALONG, DAY 5

JC: Stand firm in one spirit, with one mind striving side by side for the faith of the gospel. (Philippians 1:27 ESV)

(my reaction)

MS: We are better together, aren't we, Jesus? There is nothing like accomplishing something amazing and having another person to share it with. It's why we instantly want to "phone a friend" when we get great news. I'm amazed you let me be a part of your work, Jesus. And I'm glad to be part of a church family that is living your mission!

MS: When was the last time you celebrated with a member of God's family?

(my prayer reply to JC)

WEEK 6   WE WELCOME ALL
Acts 9:1–31

WORSHIP

Psalm 32

Today's psalm is a celebration of the journey of repentance and restoration given to us by God's grace. Read the psalm together with joy, then take a few moments to silently reflect on an example of this restoration they have seen. After a time invite any individual to state again one verse or phrase of the psalm they are relishing. Close with another round of verse 11 and an *Amen!*

Psalm 32 (NLT)

> ¹*Oh, what joy for those*
>   *whose disobedience is forgiven,*
>   *whose sin is put out of sight!*
>
> ²*Yes, what joy for those*
>   *whose record the L*ORD *has cleared of guilt,*
>   *whose lives are lived in complete honesty!*
>
> ³*When I refused to confess my sin,*
>   *my body wasted away,*
>   *and I groaned all day long.*
>
> ⁴*Day and night your hand of discipline was heavy on me.*
>   *My strength evaporated like water in the summer heat.*   *Interlude*
>
> ⁵*Finally, I confessed all my sins to you*
>   *and stopped trying to hide my guilt.*
> *I said to myself, "I will confess my rebellion to the L*ORD.*"*
>   *And you forgave me! All my guilt is gone.*   *Interlude*
>
> ⁶*Therefore, let all the godly pray to you while there is still time,*
>   *that they may not drown in the floodwaters of judgment.*
>
> ⁷*For you are my hiding place;*
>   *you protect me from trouble.*
>   *You surround me with songs of victory.*   *Interlude*

⁸The Lord says, "I will guide you along the best pathway
  for your life.
  I will advise you and watch over you.
⁹Do not be like a senseless horse or mule
  that needs a bit and bridle to keep it under control."
¹⁰Many sorrows come to the wicked,
  but unfailing love surrounds those who trust the Lord.
¹¹So rejoice in the Lord and be glad, all you who obey him!
  Shout for joy, all you whose hearts are pure!

VIDEO

Notes:

We are called to extend _____*love*_____ and _____*hospitality*_____ to all.

Trinity Family Values

Serve
Leading
Sharing

God had a plan for her ... all it took was an invitation from a _____*friend*_____ *and*_____, a _____*small group*_____ that listened, and a whole lot of _____*prayer*_____.

DISCUSSION

This week we're jumping back to the ninth chapter of Acts to see the entry point of Saul/Paul into the mission of the church. We've already seen Paul in action as a leading force in spreading the message of Jesus. Last weekend's sermon told us how inclusive Paul's message was, even to the man holding him in jail in Philippi. Now we want to see where Paul first experienced this remarkable, merciful inclusion as a foundational characteristic of Good News. Rather than reading the whole text this week, we're going to read it one chunk at a time.

Read Acts 9:1–9. Saul (also known by his Greek name Paul) is first introduced at the execution of Stephen serving as the official coat holder for those carrying out the execution. (Acts 7:58) He next carries out house to house searches persecuting believers in Jerusalem. (Acts 8:3) Now in Acts 9:1–9 Saul hits the road to reach beyond Jerusalem with arrest warrants that will result in more executions.

- Put yourself in Saul's sandals and trace his state of mind through each frame of this storyboard; Jerusalem, on the road, in Damascus. Use the emojis if helpful.

Now let's focus more closely on Ananias, the man God chose to have first contact with Saul. Read Acts 9:10–19 and recognize how he must wrestle with the directions he has been given.

- Sift through the barriers he must face in welcoming Saul. Dig deep. Barriers have deep, hidden roots.
- Which ones do you particularly identify with?

Ananias is not only an example of the challenge to love our enemies, but the depth of trust required in the redemptive power of the Gospel.

- Make a list of people groups you might consider to be outside of the church box, people beyond redemption.
- What fear is rooted in each example?
- Is a personal hurt at the root of your love-ability?
- Has this conversation called a name or face to mind… someone you should include in your **Two Plus** prayers or make **Level 1 Contact?**

Now stretch a bit to shift viewpoints. What people group(s) might consider themselves to be outside of the church box.

- What fear may be rooted in their perspective?
- What might an authentic invitation include?
- What would it take for them to feel welcome?

2. Ask yourself, "Who are the unexpected people in my life that God is calling me to reach?"

- Would it be best to approach them with an invitation to a church service, a small group study session, a social event, or a personal social connection with you?
- What would it look like for you to extend this kind of welcome to a specific person you know? Rehearse. Pray together about these opportunities.

Read Acts 9:20–31. Paul's journey from verse 1 to verse 31 is an act of God, not proof of Ananias' eloquence. His encounter with Jesus, and his experience of graceful acceptance have been transformative and have a far-reaching effect.

- How does this encourage you to broaden your welcoming horizon? *anything is possible*
- Where have you seen the Gospel bring transformation in the life of someone unexpected?
- Where could the Gospel reach if you interacted with one of those people groups you listed above?
- If your path currently does not intersect with someone in one of those groups, what would it take to put yourself in their location... a vision? Listen carefully if someone in your group is feeling a nudge from the Holy Spirit about this. Discuss possible steps very concretely. Pray together about it now and check-in for further prayer in some weeks to follow.

CLOSING

The leader will pass out prayer cards and give instruction for today's litany prayer.

Responses adapted from Psalm 32 (CEV).

Leader: Heavenly Father, in Christ you have gathered us all together here, many people from many walks of life.
Group: You are our secret hideout! You protect us from trouble. You surround us with songs of rescue!

Leader: You long to gather all peoples. You're love for those who are still far away from you remains.
Group: The one whose wrongdoing is forgiven, whose sin is covered over, is truly happy!

Leader: We pray that we would be an open family in you; open to all peoples that you have called home. We pray for the following groups of people:

(Take a moment to pray for all the groups of people identified during the study time as listed on your card.)

Leader: Your Word teaches us the faithful should pray to you during troubled times (verse 6), so we lift up these requests that weigh on our hearts.

(Take a moment to pray for all the prayer requests of the group as listed on your card.)

Leader: You who are righteous, rejoice in the Lord and be glad!
Group: All you whose hearts are right, sing out in joy!

Leader: We pray in the name of the one Son.
All: Amen.

WEEK 6 PRAYER NOTES PAGE

TWO **PLUS**

TODAY'S TEXT: WE WELCOME ALL, DAY 1

JC: After this I looked, and behold, a great multitude that no one could number, from every nation, from all tribes and peoples and languages, standing before the throne and before the Lamb, clothed in white robes, with palm branches in their hands.
(Revelation 7:9 ESV)

(my reaction)

GP: Heaven is going to be an amazing place. But what about now? People hurt each other, believe in nothing that I do and are hateful in both word and deeds. You want me to get in the middle of that? I could be embarrassed, humiliated, scorned or hurt. I'm afraid I can't do this on my own.

GP: Who do you think of as different or unapproachable or unlikely to be found in heaven?

(my prayer reply to JC)

TODAY'S TEXT: WE WELCOME ALL, DAY 2

JC: There is neither Jew nor Greek, slave nor free, male nor female, for you are all one in Christ Jesus. (Galatians 3:28 ESV)

(my reaction)

GP: When you get down to it, we are all the same. We all have the same basic needs. We all want life to have meaning and purpose; to believe in something greater than ourselves. With your help Jesus, I am able to give an answer to everyone who asks to give a reason for the hope I have in you.

GP: What is a reason for the hope that you have in Jesus?

(my prayer reply to JC)

TODAY'S TEXT: WE WELCOME ALL, DAY 3

JC: If you love only those who love you, what reward is there for that? Even corrupt tax collectors do that much. If you are kind only to your friends, how are you different from anyone else? Even pagans do that. But you are to be perfect, even as your Father in heaven is perfect. (Matthew 5:46–48 NLT)

(my reaction)

GP: I understand. If I stay in my comfort zone, I'm just being like everyone else and no one sees Jesus in me. It's when I step out and rely on God, and not on my own strength that I can live a life of generosity and graciousness to everyone.

GP: Is there a barrier (prejudice, fear, attitude) that is keeping you from reaching out to people God has put into your life?

(my prayer reply to JC)

TODAY'S TEXT: WE WELCOME ALL, DAY 4

JC: Therefore, accept each other just as Christ has accepted you so that God will be given glory. (Romans 15:7 NLT)

(my reaction)

GP: I forget—I didn't accept you, but you accepted me. I forget—I was lost, but you saved me, not because of anything I did, but because of everything you did. Help me get past my fear of reaching out to someone not like me. I want to feel the joy that comes from knowing you are glorified by my faithfulness.

GP: What is one step you can make to accept someone who is not like you?

(my prayer reply to JC)

TODAY'S TEXT: WE WELCOME ALL, DAY 5

JC: And I have other sheep that are not of this fold. I must bring them also, and they will listen to my voice. So there will be one flock, one shepherd. (John 10:16 ESV)

(my reaction)

😍 😎 😉 😮 😢

GP: I was once not in the fold either. You weren't satisfied Lord with leaving me out there on my own. You put people in my life who brought me to you and who helped to nurture my faith; like Paul had Silas. Now I get the privilege to be that person for others. I'm grateful you've given me so many ways to do this through my church family; small groups, mission trips, serving opportunities. Use me as you see fit so I can help you grow the flock.

GP: Who can you partner with to make a difference in someone's life? Is there a service team at Trinity you want to join?

(my prayer reply to JC)

WEEK 7 WE GIVE SACRIFICIALLY
Acts 4:32–5:11

WORSHIP

Today you're invited to combine your weekly "catch-up" with some praise for God. You'll see the psalm below is divided into 3 paragraphs. Assign a reader for each one. After one section is read, ask if someone would volunteer a praise connection from life this week pertinent to that section. Ask everyone to respond with a verse 13 "Bless the Lord..." and move on to the next section.

Psalm 41 (TLB)

¹ God blesses those who are kind to the poor. He helps them out of their troubles. ² He protects them and keeps them alive; he publicly honors them and destroys the power of their enemies. ³ He nurses them when they are sick and soothes their pains and worries.

(a voiced praise connection)

Trinity Family Values

Serve
Generosity
Accountability

¹³ Bless the Lord, the God of Israel, who exists from everlasting ages past—and on into everlasting eternity ahead.

⁴ "O Lord," I prayed, "be kind and heal me, for I have confessed my sins." ⁵ But my enemies say, "May he soon die and be forgotten!" ⁶ They act so friendly when they come to visit me while I am sick; but all the time they hate me and are glad that I am lying there upon my bed of pain. And when they leave, they laugh and mock. ⁷ They whisper together about what they will do when I am dead. ⁸ "It's fatal, whatever it is," they say. "He'll never get out of that bed!"

(a voiced praise connection)

¹³ *Bless the Lord, the God of Israel, who exists from everlasting ages past—and on into everlasting eternity ahead.*

⁹ *Even my best friend has turned against me—a man I completely trusted; how often we ate together.* ¹⁰ *Lord, don't you desert me! Be gracious, Lord, and make me well again so I can pay them back!* ¹¹ *I know you are pleased with me because you haven't let my enemies triumph over me.* ¹² *You have preserved me because I was honest; you have admitted me forever to your presence.*

(a voiced praise connection)

¹³ *Bless the Lord, the God of Israel, who exists from everlasting ages past—and on into everlasting eternity ahead.*

VIDEO

Notes:

_____ stirred their hearts to be generous.

They gave _____ by selling their most valuable things.

They laid this at the feet of their leaders, _____

_____ to use the proceeds wisely.

Those leaders gave from these gifts to those who were _____

_____.

Pause to read Acts 5:1–5:11 aloud.

God takes sin _____.

They missed a chance to be _____ _____ by being generous.

Our giving should always be _____...

It should be done _____...

It should be done _____.

_____ may be the greatest struggle we face as believers in our society today.

DISCUSSION

Acts 4:32–38 describes the actions of the church. Note—Joseph/Barnabas is the same Barnabas we've already met in session 5 & 6.

- What is the *why* behind those actions?
- Where could this community spirit possibly have come from?
- Check out Deuteronomy 15:4–11 to find the Old Testament roots for Barnabas' action. How would you describe the family value God is setting up for his people?
- Where have you seen other indications of a generous spirit in Barnabas these last weeks?

Acts 5:1–11 introduces Ananias and Sapphira, husband and wife, members of the Christian community in Jerusalem. This story often raises a "whoa" 😳 response from people. It's not just a story about honesty. It goes deeper into integrity not just of the individual but how the integrity of the whole faith family is impacted.

- What could be Ananias' motivation for keeping a portion of his profits?
- What could be Sapphira's?
- Contrast their Family Values with those of Barnabas.

But if anyone has the world's goods and sees his brother in need, yet closes his heart against him, how does God's love abide in him? 1 John 3:17 (ESV)

- John reflects the same family value of Deuteronomy (above) in 1 John 3:17. How would you answer the question that John raises?

Pastor Mark described this early church as—**Generous**—sacrificial givers—**trusting** the leadership's use of the funds—**meeting real needs** of individuals.

- How does Ananias and Sapphira contradict each of these?

Let's dig a bit to see why God takes sin seriously.

> *Here are six things God hates, and one more that he loathes with a passion:*
> *eyes that are arrogant,*
> *a tongue that lies,*
> *hands that murder the innocent,*
> *a heart that hatches evil plots,*
> *feet that race down a wicked track,*
> *a mouth that lies under oath,*
> *a troublemaker in the family.*   Proverbs 6:16–19 (MSG)

The six-plus-one language at the beginning is a hint to look closely at the first six values listed and the conclusion of the seventh. An individual's actions go beyond the individual. They impact not only the peace of the family but the impact the family has in the larger community. Support this conclusion with a brief "such as" scenario for each of the six.

- Can you connect any of these actions to Ananias and Sapphira?
- How might the credibility and witness of the early church been impacted?

Both verse 5 and 11 of Acts 5 uses the word *fear/phobos* which contains the concept of profound respect. Look for the concept here in Paul's message to the church at Philippi.

> *Dear friends, you always followed my instructions when I was with you. And now that I am away, it is even more important. Work hard to show the results of your salvation, obeying God with deep reverence and fear. For God is work-*

ing in you, giving you the desire and the power to do what pleases him. Philippians 2:12–13 (NLT) 😴

- How does profound respect for God move you to an active faith? Give examples.
- How does it enter your decisions about financially supporting the ministry of the church?

Notice how this foundation of profound respect for God is followed by amazing things, Acts 5:12–16.

A Tithing Conversation

- When you make a pledge to tithe, or any other portion of pledged financial commitment, which is the basis for your later decision to fulfill your commitment?
  - Respect for God
  - Integrity in your relationship with Him
  - The integrity of Trinity in meeting our shared financial commitments
  - None of the above 😜
- What in your practice of stewardship is
  - Intentional
  - Cheerful
  - Willing
- Who have you seen model that kind of stewardship?

When you can meet someone's tangible need you are not only blessing them, but you feel the blessing of God's Spirit grow in your own heart. You're feeling the smile of God on your loving response to another. God's joy becomes the joy of all involved.

- How have you experienced generosity as a blessing personally?
- How have you seen that generosity blessing play out at Trinity?

Now let's get real about Ananias and Sapphira's decision. They held back to provide their own nest egg, not trusting God's provision or the church's care should they fall into need.

- How does your self-reliance for tomorrow's expenses affect your ability to be generous?
- What steps would be an incremental way for you to grow in your trust for God's provision?
- What do you know about Trinity's processes for helping people with their needs? Assign someone in the group to find out and report back.

Another motivator for Ananias and Sapphira was their status in this generous church community. Our net worth is often a key component in our opinion of our own self-worth. It also shapes our opinions of others. 😎 😎

- What is the basis of our opinion of each other in the church?

Sometimes we don't see another person's needs because we confuse our own wants with needs. We feel that what we have is never enough and don't see that the bounty God has provided is to be shared.

- How does materialism create a barrier to other areas of your walk with God; ie. studying God's Word, prayer, caring for others, serving at Trinity?
- How would an adjustment in lifestyle allow you to be generous?
- How can your group support your decision and your follow through?
- Pray for the concerns raised right now.

Here are some financial planning tools available for individuals. Contact Marge.Franzen@tlc4u.org for more information on how to get connected.

- *Generosity Ladder*—a thoughtful podcast walking through the spiritual steps toward God's idea of generosity. Also available as a booklet.
- *Financial Peace University*—a comprehensive course on personal financial management available as a class or individually on line.

- Personal Budget Planning—One-on-one help getting a budget in place.
- *Transfer the Blessings*—Free assistance in benevolent gift and estate planning by the LCMS Foundation.

CLOSING

Psalm 41

Responses adapted from Psalm 41 (CEV) as responses to the Lord's Prayer.

Leader: Our Father who art in heaven,
Group: Bless the Lord, the God of Israel, from forever to forever!

Leader: Hallowed be your name,
Group: Amen and Amen!

Leader: Your kingdom come,
Group: please have mercy on us and lift us up.

Leader: Your will be done on earth as it is in heaven.
Group: Those who pay close attention to the poor are truly happy!

Leader: Give us this day our daily bread;
Group: The Lord protects us and keeps us alive;

Leader: Forgive us our sins as we forgive those who sin against us;
Group: "Lord, have mercy on me! Heal me because I have sinned against you."

Leader: Lead us not into temptation,
Group: You support me in my integrity.

Leader: Deliver us from evil.
Group: You put me in your presence forever.

    All: Thine is the kingdom and the power and the glory forever and ever. Amen.

WEEK 7 PRAYER NOTES PAGE

TWO **PLUS**

TODAY'S TEXT: WE GIVE SACRIFICIALLY, DAY 1

JC: If any of you needs wisdom to know what you should do, you should ask God, and he will give it to you. God is generous to everyone and doesn't find fault with them. (James 1:5 GW)

(my reaction)

😀 😉 😌 😊

MF: Hey! Everything we know about generosity comes from God's generosity with us! I don't have to match up or pay up. I just want to learn from the Master. He's generous every which way supplying truth, wisdom, rescue, provision.

MF: What would you put on God's generosity list when you consider your life?

(my prayer reply to JC)

TODAY'S TEXT: WE GIVE SACRIFICIALLY, DAY 2

JC: Each of you should give whatever you have decided. You shouldn't be sorry that you gave or feel forced to give, since God loves a cheerful giver. (2 Corinthians 9:7 GW)

(my reaction)

MF: Oh, guess I have to actually put some thought into my own generosity and avoid both regrets and peer pressure. I have to see and understand the needs that I can supply. Deciding ahead gives me the discipline of commitment and the challenge of follow through. The routine of giving opens the door for God honoring cheerfulness.

MF: How is my heart responding to the needs for Trinity's mission and the needs of Trinity's people? How can I make my giving systematic?

(my prayer reply to JC)

TODAY'S TEXT: WE GIVE SACRIFICIALLY, DAY 3

JC: The generous will prosper; those who refresh others will themselves be refreshed. (Proverbs 11:25 NLT)

(my reaction)

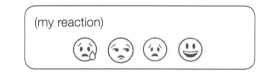

MF: Writing that Trinity check every week can feel like a pinch, mostly because of my fear of the bill pile. You're saying, "I've got this!" I guess I can't outdo your generosity.

MF: Pinpoint the pinch adjustment to your budget that would be needed for a regular tithe and apply a good portion of trust in God. What do you see as a possible outcome for others?

(my prayer reply to JC)

TODAY'S TEXT: WE GIVE SACRIFICIALLY, DAY 4

JC: Tell those who have the riches of this world not to be arrogant and not to place their confidence in anything as uncertain as riches. Instead, they should place their confidence in God who richly provides us with everything to enjoy. Tell them to do good, to do a lot of good things, to be generous, and to share. By doing this they store up a treasure for themselves which is a good foundation for the future. In this way they take hold of what life really is. (1 Timothy 6:17–19 GW)

(my reaction)

MF: I'm seeing that the decisions about giving are a learning process. It's not about how much I think should be in my bank account now. It's about the journey I'm taking in God's Kingdom. Confidence in taking these steps rests in my confidence in God.

MF: Which is my step towards a consistent tithe offering?
- Give my heart to the need.
- Practice consistency.
- Set it into my budget before other allotments.
- Adjust my instant gratification spending so more is available.

(my prayer reply to JC)

TODAY'S TEXT: WE GIVE SACRIFICIALLY, DAY 5

JC: God gives seed to the farmer and food to those who need to eat. God will also give you seed and multiply it. In your lives he will increase the things you do that have his approval.
(2 Corinthians 9:10 GW)

(my reaction)

MF: Amazing! The farmer invests some seeds and up comes meals for many. I've got some "seed" to plant from our Generous God and He's going to generously produce what's needed by many. Sounds like a challenge… sounds like an adventure!

MF: Who can I ask to hold me accountable to the way I plant my "seed"? Who helps me hone my skills and be faithful in my daily energy investment? Who helps me find the best needs to meet with my harvest? Who watches that I stick to the plan?

(my prayer reply to JC)

WEEK 8   WE REACH OUT WITH THE GOOD NEWS

WORSHIP

Psalm 66

Read the psalm together out loud, one verse at a time around the circle of your group, a variety of translations is fine reflecting the variety of people in your group. Leave a little time between each verse to enjoy and smile at God. After reading, reflect together on the ways God has blessed your time together as a group. Finish off with one more "Thanks be to God!" ☺

VIDEO

(Pause video to read Acts 17:16–34 together when prompted.)

Trinity Family Values

Sharing

Accountability

Notes:

Paul is keenly aware of a

_____

_____ in the culture.

Paul _____

who "happened to be there."

Paul receives _____

faith from those in his culture.

Paul shares his faith in simple, straight-forward terms, _____

_____.

Paul points the way _____ (not to himself)

as he finishes sharing his faith.

DISCUSSION

Use these discussion aides to unpack Pastor Mike's points.

1. **Paul is keenly aware of a spiritual need in the culture (because they worshiped idols).**

   Acts 17:16   Issues try to take God's place, and any issue we face in life that takes God's place becomes an idol. People can worry themselves into spiritual submission. They search for their own source of wisdom which often ends up as silent as that stone god at the Areopagus that doesn't move, think, speak, or feel. Paul addresses this need for spiritual connection.

   - How can we become more aware of what our culture worships instead of God?
   - What issue is God bringing to your attention these days? What element of idolatry—disconnection from or defamation of God—lurks within that issue? ☹
   - Who do you go to when voicing your concerns and discouragement over our post-Christian culture?

2. **Paul interacts with people who "happened to be there."**

   Acts 17:17-18   The pervasive presence of idolatry spurs Paul into action. He goes to the synagogue and presses the local Jewish population as well as the Gentile God-fearing converts, the people most like him. Yet he cannot rest and pursues an audience in the marketplace filled with government buildings, offices, shops, food, art, plazas… and altars.

   - What would be the modern parallel to the Athens marketplace?
   - Who in your life happens to be in your marketplace, but you now know they are there by God's design?
   - Have you taken a tour of your neighborhood, your local marketplace, the city center around your workplace, or even the neighborhood around your worship site? Make it a prayer walk, asking the Holy Spirit to open your eyes and pick up clues about what drives the people around you. Do

this regularly seeking God's leading. Discuss the possibility of making such a prayer walk a group activity. Find directions for a Trinity site prayer walk in the Appendix.

3. Paul receives invitations to share faith from those in his culture.

Acts 17:18-21   The Greek Stoics and Epicureans would have felt right at home in the 21st century. Notice their openness to ideas and discussion. Just because someone believes differently doesn't mean they won't be open for a conversation.

- Where are you being invited into the lives of others? Remember God is the designer of our life's journey. This may appear to be an accidental crossing of paths or a new turn in the conversation with someone you know. Add them to your **Two Plus** list. Ask the group to pray for them as you see new stages in your relationship developing. Right now, pray together for an opening in your conversations that leads to an introduction of Jesus.

- When you move into **Level 2 Contact** or start looking at existing relationships as a call to be on God's mission, you are embarking on a long journey. Discuss ways the group can stay in touch and continue to support each other even while you're not meeting weekly as a group.

4. Paul shares his faith in simple, straight-forward terms, without holding back.

Acts 17:22-34   Paul's sermon in Athens is different from other sermons we find in Acts. Paul is putting in themes that will connect with the audience while still being true to the Good News of Jesus, but he makes no assumptions about using "faith" vocabulary.

- What are some key parts of the Gospel message that you heard?
- What kind of language do you use each day with others, and why?
- What faith terms do you think they would not understand?

- What components of your faith do you think would be conversation stoppers?

5. Paul points the way to Jesus (not to himself) as he finishes sharing his faith.
- How is the Good News of Jesus still relevant today?
- What truth about Jesus do you think would be most winsome in the ears of the person mentioned in the Point 3 discussion?

To understand what you can expect when entering into a faith conversation, scan through the text again and note who Receives, who Rejects, and who Requests in their response to Paul's message.

You may be asking, "How do I boldly shape my faithful representation of Jesus and his Good News in a way that is relevant without pulling any punches about God's truth?" Here are what Bill Hybels calls Irreducible Ingredients in Sharing Good News in his book *Just Walk Across the Room:* 😃

1. God loves you—Matthew 18:14
2. Christ chose to pay for you (we can't save ourselves)
3. The choice is now yours… how will you respond to God's offer of love?

As a group familiarize yourselves with these and discuss why they are "irreducible."

Again, thinking of the person in Point 3, how would you shape your words around these ingredients?

CLOSING

Responses adapted from Psalm 66 (CEV).

Leader: Heavenly Father, our lives are given to you. You have redeemed us by the blood of Jesus and restored us to you.

Group: Sing praises to the glory of God's name! Make glorious his praise!

Leader: Yet, all too often, idols of our own making dominate our lives.

Group: **But you brought us out to freedom! So I'll enter your house.**

Leader: We seek to be your witnesses to the ends of the earth, Lord. But too often we see these same idols controlling those around us. We pray for the words to speak into those cultures.

Group: **Come and see God's deeds; his works for human beings are awesome.**

Leader: Too often we see those around us as random passers-by rather than people placed into our lives to hear your Gospel from us.

Group: **I will tell them what God has done for me.**

Leader: As we live our lives in you, Lord, we know there will be people around us that see us. We pray for the moments when they invite us to share our testimonies with them.

Group: **Bless God! He didn't reject my prayer; he didn't withhold his faithful love from me.**

Leader: And when those moments arise we pray for what Peter instructed of us, to always be ready to give the reason for the hope that we have. (1 Peter 3:15)

Group: **All you nations, bless our God! Let the sound of his praise be heard!**

Leader: As we share Lord, we pray that we would point the way only to our redeemer, your son, Jesus.

Group: **All the earth worships you, sings praises to you, sings praises to your name!**

Leader: Let our testimony to the world be praises to your holy name. We pray this in your son's name.

Group: **God definitely listened. He heard the sound of our prayer.**

All: **Amen... Amen!**

WEEK 8 PRAYER NOTES PAGE

TWO **PLUS**

TODAY'S TEXT: WE REACH OUT WITH THE GOOD NEWS, DAY 1

JC: I am not ashamed of the gospel, for it is the power of God for salvation to everyone who believes. (Romans 1:16 ESV)

(my reaction)

MS: If I focus on the faults and the failings of the family of God on earth, I find it easy to be ashamed. Christians can be judgmental. Churches teach and do stupid things. A lot of bad stuff has been done in the name of religion. But if I focus on the Good News about Jesus, God's love and power to save, then I can be bold for you, Jesus!

MS: When have you seen God's power at work in your life?

(my prayer reply to JC)

TODAY'S TEXT: WE REACH OUT WITH THE GOOD NEWS, DAY 2

JC: I heard the voice of the Lord saying, "Whom shall I send, and who will go for us?" Then I said, "Here I am! Send me."
(Isaiah 6:8 ESV)

(my reaction)

MS: Me, Jesus. Send me. Send me even though I know I still have a lot of growing up to do. Send me even when I am afraid. Send me even when I am more focused on my own agenda than yours. Send me despite all the other things in my life that seem to be more important. Send me… because there are people I love who are far from you.

MS: What is keeping you from giving yourself fully to His mission?

(my prayer reply to JC)

TODAY'S TEXT: WE REACH OUT WITH THE GOOD NEWS, DAY 3

JC: Go into all the world and proclaim the gospel to the whole creation. (Mark 16:15 ESV)

(my reaction)

MS: "Into all the world"—sounds fun! Maybe I should go on a short-term mission trip to some far-away place. Or send money to support a missionary in Africa. Or at least volunteer once a month at a soup kitchen in the city. Just don't send me to be a missionary where I work. Or at the health club. Or in my neighborhood. Those places are scary!

MS: What gets in the way of you sharing the Gospel in familiar places?

(my prayer reply to JC)

TODAY'S TEXT: WE REACH OUT WITH THE GOOD NEWS, DAY 4

JC: Always being prepared to make a defense to anyone who asks you for a reason for the hope that is in you; yet do it with gentleness and respect. (1 Peter 3:15 ESV)

(my reaction)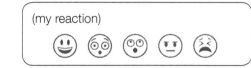

MS: There are two things about that that make me pause, Jesus. First, I don't always show my hope to others. I let circumstances of this life overwhelm my hope. Forgive me. And when I do have a chance to share my hope… it's hard to respect what others believe. They believe some pretty crazy stuff! Help me to listen, to love, and to care.

MS: How has following Jesus changed your life? What would you say if someone actually asked you that question?

(my prayer reply to JC)

TODAY'S TEXT: WE REACH OUT WITH THE GOOD NEWS, DAY 5

JC: And pray for me, too. Ask God to give me the right words so I can boldly explain God's mysterious plan that the Good News is for Jews and Gentiles alike. (Ephesians 6:19 NLT)

(my reaction)

MS: Being a member of God's family is NOT safe. People who think Christianity is for the weak aren't doing it right. Sharing the Good News of God's love and truth is risky and frightening. Yet history is filled with the stories of people who have boldly risked all for the Gospel. Lord, give me that kind of boldness!

MS: What bold thing is God calling you to do today? This week? This year? Who is going to support you in that step?

(my prayer reply to JC)

VIDEO NOTES ANSWER KEY

WEEK 1

Being part of the family can be **frustrating**.

"**Family**" is one of the main ways that God describes his church.

People sharing their **hearts**

They loved each other because **Jesus told them to**.

WEEK 2

This family of God were **led** by the Holy Spirit.

They were led by being daily in **God's Word**, daily in **prayer**, and by doing it **together**.

Are we open to **discover** the greater work God wants to do through us?

WEEK 3

God takes **ordinary** people and uses them in **extraordinary** ways.

Sometimes we seek to get our **prayers answered** by striking a deal with God.

God will use the supernatural power of his **Spirit** for his **mission**.

His primary goal is to align our **hearts** with his.

WEEK 4

Know the Good News of Jesus Christ will cause **division**.

Know that following Jesus means I must be **authentic**.

Know that you are not **alone**; this is US, not this is YOU.

WEEK 5

When two or more people interact for a long enough time, **conflict happens**.

Is it possible that the disagreement, which brought about a split, was a **good** thing, the **best** outcome?

WEEK 6

We are called to extend **love** and **hospitality** to all.

God had a plan for her ... all it took was an invitation from a **friend**, a **small group** that listened, and a whole lot of **prayer**.

WEEK 7

God stirred their hearts to be generous.

They gave **sacrificially** by selling their most valuable things.

They laid this at the feet of their leaders, **trusting them** to use the proceeds wisely.

Those leaders gave from these gifts to those who were **in need**.

God takes sin **seriously**.

They missed a chance to be **blessed** by being generous.

Our giving should always be **intentional**... It should be done **cheerfully**... It should be done **willingly**.

Materialism may be the greatest struggle we face as believers in our society today.

WEEK 8

Paul is keenly aware of a **spiritual need** in the culture.

Paul **interacts with people** who "happened to be there."

Paul receives **invitations to share** faith from those in his culture.

Paul shares his faith in simple, straight-forward terms, **without holding back**.

Paul points the way **to Jesus** (not to himself) as he finishes sharing his faith.

THIS IS US LEADER'S NOTES

Check out Trinity's *Connect* Family Value:

Connect—We are in small group communities.

Those small groups are healthy, meaning they study the Word, are coached in and connected to Trinity's mission, and meet regularly.

As a group leader, you are vital to the mission Trinity has embarked on with the leading of the Holy Spirit. It is a joy to see how God continues to bless people through the connections of small groups gathered around His Word. We pray that the Spirit plants and grows that same joy in your heart as the weeks of the series flow and you live life together.

- We ask that you do some Spirit-directed dreaming about who would be served by being in your group and give direct invitations.
- We ask that you pray daily for the individuals in your group and ask the Holy Spirit to grow your heart and care for them.
- We ask that you be faithful in your prep time for each session. Each session has been scoped with a wide range of groups in mind. Find your group's best path by selecting or even rephrasing questions. Please budget your time so you get to the portion that addresses our personal function as part of God's family and part of God's mission. If your group shares the facilitating role, be in contact between sessions and collaborate on the best approach for the group.
- We ask that you personally reflect on Trinity's Family Values and consider how you can reflect them as you lead the group.
- We ask that you keep an eye out for the hand of God in the lives of your group members and encourage them in the steps they are being led toward not only in group session conversation but also with personal contact.

Your coach will be in contact with you during the trimester, staying in touch with you and sending you tips. You can rely on them for any kind of support you need as a group leader. Feel free to contact them before they contact you! Be sure to give them a prayer update week by week for you and for your group.

In the Appendix, you'll find tips for setting your group up in Planning Center Groups where registrations will be open. This group site will also give you email tools and attendance keeping functions. Check out the instructions and contact your coach for assistance. Who's your coach?

Trinity Galewood
- Zach Gates (zach.gates@tlc4u.org)

Trinity Green Trails
- Tony Dieckmann (tony.dieckmann@tlc4u.org)
- Dan Grissom (dan.grissom@tlc4u.org)

Trinity Kimberly Way
- Dennis Franzen (dennis.franzen@tlc4u.org)
- Nick Price (nick.price@tlc4u.org)

Trinity South Naperville
- Mike Curtis (mike.curtis@tlc4u.org)

WEEK 1 LEADER'S NOTES

Check to make sure everyone in your group has a book a week before your session. Ask them to read the introduction to the study on pages 1–5 as an appetizer before you get together for your first session. Check that your DVD runs in your equipment for the video introduction to each session. You can also stream the video from www.tlc4u.org/ThisIsUs.

This first week is the best time to get the ball rolling on your group serve. Our weServe team has planned some serving events for October and November, but if you want to jump into our partnership with Feed My Starving Children for the Live the Love pack event we recommend you register your group members and any guests as soon as possible. (See information in the Appendix) You'll find information about all your options at www/tlc4u.org/makeadifference—where you can look for current serving options any time. Pick one that matches your group's gifts and heart or create your own way to serve a neighbor or your community and make a difference.

Your session opens with worship using a psalm. Read the introduction and follow the directions to simply enter into the presence of God with a heart filled with praise and thanksgiving. Refrain from searching for connections to the Acts study text. Let the Spirit draw you to God before you get into study mode.

This session discusses commitments and the family nature of the relationships your group will be developing these next eight weeks. As you discuss how the Acts 2 church practiced their commitments in their cultural context and their Jerusalem location, let the group have freedom in finding how to transfer those ideas to your culture and location proposing group commitments. At some point, however, you want to arrive at an agreement of under what commitments and expectations the group will operate. Where do we meet, for how long, with or without food, with or without kids, confidentiality, consistent attendance, open for invites, social gatherings. Some groups will get formal and write expectations out. Some groups operate less formally. Some groups have been together for a while and have a long-term understanding while others are at the first stage of relationship. But in all cases the agreement should be clear to all. As the eight weeks unfold, group life may get a little wobbly. You can point to this agreement to regain a firm footing.

At the end of the session have everyone turn to page 12 to find the devotional material provided for them as Today's Text. Clarify that the five daily readings for the first week would start on the day after your first session. These readings were selected for their further personal processing and prayer on the theme of the session.

Before your group members go out the door this week (or alternatively send them all an email or text next Saturday) remind them to keep an eye out at next weekend's service for someone they don't know. Encourage them to make an introduction and invite them to session two.

WEEK 2 LEADER'S NOTES

As you go through the first few sessions you'll be establishing a group norm for open sharing, willingness to pray and be prayed for, how deep to dive, and how to stay on track. This is part of the fine art of leading a group, something you learn as you go, but please—do not fail to pray constantly over your group session as you prepare and as you are in session. What happens in the session is in God's hands. Watch for it! Thank Him for it!

One of the "artful" parts of leading this curriculum is the Trinity Family Values found each week in a family picture frame. They've been selected for their connection to the session. There is no scripted conversation. Keep your ears tuned for one of the values in each session's box to surface in your group's discussion and simply point it out. Another tactic could be to assign each of the framed values in the box to someone as spotter for the session.

This week's session makes some assumptions about your group's understanding of the Holy Spirit and what it means to listen to the Spirit. The groundwork for this is laid in the week two *This Is Us* sermon. Take notes in service or review it on tlc4u.org/sermons and be prepared to recap as needed for your group.

The Trinity Family Value of *Sharing* is a thread that runs through several sessions as we examine the mission of the church in Acts. This session marks some first steps in forming an attitude and a plan for our individual life in the mission of the church. Be sure to make a start this week in the final section of this week's session, but understand there will be continued development through the eight sessions. Watch for any individual's progress and adjust your personal prayers for them throughout the series. Point your group to the Two Plus section of the prayer notes page and the additional resources in the Appendix: **Level 1 and 2 Contacts, Simple Ways to be Missional.**

The subject of discernment over a major decision is often an issue that arises in a person's life, one that they carry to their group. **Finding God's Will Together** is a resource in the Appendix. If you don't need it for this trimester, you may need it at another time in your group's life together.

WEEK 3 LEADER'S NOTES

Head's up! This week's session takes you scene by scene through a rather complicated story. Note that you'll do a quick read-through before the video. Dig in and have fun—but watch your time carefully so you get through all the scenes. You may need to select which of the processing bullets are best for your group. Don't miss the essential component of the power of the Holy Spirit available to us as we live out our Trinity Family Values. You may hear everything from skepticism to wonder on the subject. Again, the Sunday sermon will be a resource for you to tap. Be sure every testimonial to God's active power brought to the group gets a full hearing open to questions yet also offering affirmation and praise for God.

For this week's closing—before you begin the prayer time, or even the day before the session, collect prayer petitions from your group. In addition, during the session make notes of intercessions that come to the surface. In the responsive prayer time this week, when you reach the petition portions, ask each person to raise their petition—encourage them to know that God knows the heart behind even a single word such as "Grandma" or "job." Alternatively, you as the leader can read each prayer request one at a time. After each, the group is invited to respond using Psalm 21:13 as directed. Leave some silent space for personal silent prayer supporting each petition.

WEEK 4 LEADER'S NOTES

In this session while pressing on towards identifying the mission God is nudging us towards we also acknowledge the opposition and count the cost. This is to be brainstorming. Be prepared to give a personal example to get things going. Be sure to pray for the specific situations that come up in the conversation. If someone in your group has the spiritual gift of faith, take time to ask them how this confidence plays out in their life. Ask them to give words of encouragement to the ones with less confidence and more stress over the opposition they face for their faith.

Use the *Ways to Prepare and Practice* as a tool for individuals to gain traction on what may be a general desire to share. When they get specific, the group can offer better encouragement, better prayer support, fleshing out the basics of the Level 1 and Level 2 Contacts in the Appendix with some brainstorming. Push for details: "How would you say that?" Ask others, "How does that sound? Do you have an alternative approach?" Consider if a group social activity would be a good tool for one or two individuals in the group to use to bring their missional relationship to a new level. Add effective accountability by encouraging them to report back.

This is week four already! Be sure to check in with your coach, giving them an updated group roster and asking for whatever assistance you need. Your coach will also like to hear any highs your group has already hit upon.

WEEK 5 LEADER'S NOTES

Head's up! This week the Acts story for Sunday and our story for the session are sequential. Send a reminder to your group to listen to the sermon recording posted on tlc4u.org/sermons for review.

We get another detailed walk through the text in this session. Go through the text and notes at least once yourself to become familiar. Checking the "Paul's Journeys" Map in the back of your study Bible may also help you get oriented. The review of Paul and Barnabas' history as well as the sidebar information on John Mark may be used in different ways. A well-rooted Bible group may only need to have it for reference. A first contact with Acts group might read through it together. Form your plan of action.

"Conflicts Past" may dredge up old wounds, but they give fruitful ground for analysis and learning. Be filled with care for everyone in your group as you facilitate the discussion. Walk a neutral line 😐, but ask clarifying questions to probe for the process that was used... or was missing... in handling the conflict. Use Acts 15 as a comparison point. You cannot get through conflict without prayer. Be sure to use a lot of it in this lesson on conflict.

WEEK 6 LEADER'S NOTES

In our culture, personal boundaries are considered healthy things. But this week's story about Saul and Ananias asks us to stretch past our boundaries when God nudges us to follow his lead. Ask your group to be frank about their own discomfort levels and use the group's experiences to open the door for change, not only of the person we are in mission toward, but the changes God will bring about in us in the process. Again, do not hesitate to put specific prayer right into your discussion. The outcome of this week's session may be a shift in someone's missional planning. Praise God together for that clarity when it arrives.

One more reminder—the Appendix resources will help tool your group. Some may be at the first considerations of the Levels of Contact, some may be into building the listening component in new relationships, some may just be awakening a mission perspective of their neighborhood or workplace. Ask the group to scan the resources during the week, then make contact to find out which resource an individual is finding helpful. Ask them to share that in an email with the group. The group may want to choose a book from the reading list for study next trimester.

For the prayer time this week, collect prayer requests informally as your group assembles. Write each one down on a card or piece of notepaper. Also make a card for each of the people groups identified during the discussion. At the closing prayer, deal out the cards to individuals. Explain to your group that this week there will be a 'popcorn prayer.' Encourage each person to voice a prayer for the needs on their cards at the appropriate point in your litany prayer. Note: Praying aloud like this can be daunting for some people, encourage them that a prayer does not have to be elaborate. Rather, a simple conversational style is perfect.

WEEK 7 LEADER'S NOTES

Head's up! We've saved that touchy *Generosity* Family Value until this seventh session. Money is uncomfortable territory for discussion and this week's story in Acts has Old Testament overtones. Some prep time on your part will help you feel prepared. It's a rather detailed session so look it over and choose which bits will be most helpful for your group. Invest some prayer for individuals in the group. Ask someone (from your group or your coach) to be praying for you as you prepare and lead.

This week's lesson falls into two parts, the **Discussion** of the Acts text and a **Tithing Conversation** of our application of the Family Value of *Generosity* raised in the text. Your challenge is to navigate the first while preserving plenty of time to discuss honestly the second. Again, sift through the questions to select the ones most needed by your group. Here is some background to help prepare you to lead:

The story of Ananias and Sapphira has an Old Testament air to it and our discomfort may come from our misunderstanding of God's call, consistent throughout the Bible, to live a life of integrity as individuals and a community, under his authority, in his Kingdom. Perhaps the closest Old Testament connection is with the story of Achan in Joshua 7. In that culture Achan's right to booty after a battle would be as normal as your right to cash your paycheck. But God has invited Israel into a level of partnership in gaining control of the land that requires them to follow his directions with integrity and trust him for their future. Achan's secret stash is an attempt to secure his personal future above that of the community. Shades of Ananias and Sapphira! He does not trust God for his future. Individual action has repercussions and Achan's has tarnished the integrity of the whole family of Israel. Judgment falls on the community and they in turn are asked to hold Achan accountable.

Peter and the other believers in Jerusalem would have known this story well. They grew up knowing how seriously God takes his covenantal relationships. A lie can only destroy the integrity of the relationship and the community. They also would have heard of Jesus' loving demand of the rich man to "... *go, sell all that you have and give to the poor, and you will have treasure in heaven; and come, follow me.*" (Mark 10:21 ESV) They knew well Jesus' statements about the cost of discipleship. *[Jesus] said, "If any of you wants to be my follower, you must give up your own way, take up your cross, and follow me. If you try to hang on to your life, you will lose it. But if you give up your life for my sake and for the sake of the Good News, you will save it. And what do you benefit if you gain the whole world but lose your own soul?* (Mark 8:34–36 NLT)

These cross references for the Acts story do not lightly brush off anyone's agitation at the sudden death of two people. They call us to listen carefully and seriously consider the basis of our own decisions that put our faith into action, especially actions involving that sensitive area around our bank account.

If you're feeling personal challenges with this subject, you have an opportunity to be real and transparent, a model for your group as they wade into the subject. The goal of the session is for people to share experiences, pray for each other where next steps are chosen and help each other where assistance is needed. Use *The Generosity Ladder* tutorial found at www.tlc4u.org/ThisIsUs to help you prep for these conversations.

Be aware of someone's financial stress in the group. If you sense an uncomfortable wall rise during this session, meet with them personally and ask, with lots of love and care expressed, if there's anything they need help with, even help in getting a budget set up. Ask your coach for help walking the group through the opportunity to meet the need or support them through the Trinity Good Samaritan Fund, which has been established to meet financial needs in our Trinity Family.

WEEK 8 LEADER'S NOTES

You've been building many attitudes and tools for our *Sharing* Family Value throughout our sessions. This week's session is in many ways the culmination of everything that we've seen in the character of the early church and how we, too, are shaped as the faith Family of Trinity. In this week's opening worship celebrate the growth you've seen.

The five points in the video are sequential and cumulative but you may need to hone in on a couple of points rather than be bogged down in the process. To steward your session time steer toward three or so of these points considering where the starting point of individuals in your group might be for the challenge of reaching out with the good news. Your goal is to get to a point where everyone is confident about sharing their faith, whatever their specific point is in the process of developing a relationship and preparing their natural testimony. Give the Holy Spirit a high five when you hear someone report about a **Level 1** or **Level 2 Contact** in the discussion or refer to their **Two Plus** prayer time.

You'll find the Prayer Circle Walk that could be used by your group or by individuals for a prayer walk in the Appendix of this book. You can also download it as a document for printing at www.tlc4u.org/ThisIsUs. Select a route, check schedules, set a date. If your group is large and scheduling is a challenge, buddy up for this activity.

If you get to point three and no one in your group feels they have been sharing life with a non-Christian, go to the Appendix and talk about **Simple Ways to be Missional.** You'll find several ideas for growing new relationships in your neighborhood, workplace, or community.

Take time again, before you close to give everyone kudos for stepping up to life together under the Trinity Family Values. Is there someone in your group newly ready to make a member commitment to Trinity? Refer them to the appropriate Site Pastor. Be sure to pass on faith stories to your coach to celebrate, too. All of us on the coaching team are thanking God for the great leaders who have served so faithfully through this series.

APPENDIX

LIVE THE LOVE

Help end childhood hunger. Join in a Western Suburb FMSC packing event on November 4, 2017 to make 500,000 meals!

The Problem:
Every day, at least 6,200 children die needlessly from starvation.

A Solution:
PACK *500,000 Meals*
- Date: Saturday, November 4, 2017
- We'll need 1,000+ volunteers for the event
- Ages 6 to 100+ can participate (children accompanied by an adult)
- Geographic scope: Western Suburbs
- Multiple 2 hour shifts throughout the day
- Location: Odeum Expo Center, Villa Park IL

How Your Group Can Help:
- Donate to the event (TAX DEDUCTABLE): https://give.fmsc.org/LiveTheLove
- Donate prizes or gift cards for a raffle
- Provide volunteers to help pack—a great invite for Level 2 Contacts—register at www.tlc4u.org/makeadifference
- Provide information and contacts to other neighborhood or work networks who may want to participate

Contact: amy.narot@tlc4u.org

About FMSC (Feed My Starving Children – www.fmsc.org):
- 850 million meals shipped so far to over 70 countries (often to orphanages) since 1987
- 99.6% of shipments have safely reached their destination
- Each meal costs $.22 and is scientifically proven for starving kids as well as pregnant women
- For 9 years running, FMSC is rated in the top 1% of all charities by the Navigator rating organization

LEVEL 1 & 2 CONTACTS

Your day is filled with people. Making an initial contact and building a relational foundation are important steps to take in drawing people closer to God. Consider the people in your sphere of influence and analyze if you are at Level 1 or Level 2. Practice what you would say about your identity or follow up questions about their identity. Brainstorm about activities you could use as invitational opportunities.

Level 1:
Get to know someone's name. It is a simple exchange of names: "My name is Dave. What's yours?" Extra points if you talk to someone about identity like who are you, who they are.

- Starting a conversation with the stranger next to you in line
- Asking a cashier about their tattoo – "Nice tattoo! – Why did you get an eagle?"
- Move from name to information

Level 2:
Invite someone to something with you. The key words are *with you*. That could be church or it could be for a cup of coffee or to your kid's baseball game... whatever. The majority of people when asked to church will not show up but an invitation should always be a part of your conversations. Keep searching for an acceptable invitation.

"Be ready to speak up and tell anyone who asks why you're living the way you are and always with the utmost courtesy. "(1 Peter 3:15 MSG)

FINDING GOD'S WILL TOGETHER
(sourced from *Leadership Journal*, Fall 2012)

When you, or someone in your group is facing a big decision, stymied by several options, or stalled in a dead end, it can be helpful to see the whole group as a resource for discerning God's leading in the moment. Or sometimes the group is facing a joint decision about the future or goal of the group. Just understand that discernment isn't an instant lightning bolt, it's a process the whole group commits to for focus on the details and on God's Word with a big investment of prayer. Here are some suggestions for ingredients to use in a process when a group commits to a discerning role.

Listen Together

This is when you all take in the whole picture. The question or options are presented clearly and completely. Recount the circumstances involved. The goal is to make sure everyone has the same information. Invite questions and offer clarification. At this point, avoid debate. Here are some good ingredients for good communication:

- Settle your mind in God's presence.
- Listen with your entire self; senses, feelings, intuition, imagination, and reason to get the full picture.
- Do not interrupt.
- Speak only for yourself. Avoid generalizations.
- Listen to the whole group. If someone is hesitant to speak, invite them to speak and be heard.
- Hold your opinions lightly. Be willing to be influenced by what others say.

While listening, you are gathering as much data as possible to inform the decision. Everyone in the group is a resource for some of these elements:

- Pertinent facts, including background and financial implications
- Voices from the community
- How direction and calling would be influenced or supported

- Scripture that speaks to the issue
- How the life of Christ informs your understanding of the situation
- The fruit of the Holy Spirit that will grow in this new proposal (Galatians 5:22–26)
- How this will draw you or others to God, or away from God
- A guiding principle from the past
- The pursuit of love for others and unity

Listen in Silence

At some point the discussion may run out of steam indicating an unclear frame of mind or it may begin to chart out a solution. Either way, take time to pause for some silence together, setting the discussion to the side while resting in God, whose Spirit is working on your hearts and minds. This gives the Spirit an opportunity to confirm a common conclusion or raise additional questions and concerns.

Reconvene and Listen Together Again

Ask what God said to them in the silence, what thoughts clarified or confused the issue, what emotions bubbled, what scripture passages came to mind. As a path becomes clear, commit to it. If two options are still in contention, discuss what could be done to improve one or the other. At this point the group may need further time apart to pray and weigh the options individually. Set a date and time to continue.

Agree Together

Bring the group back together. Trust that God will lead you to a common mind pointing to the best path that is open. Everyone may agree or there may be some reservations, but the group has heard them and everyone can move forward in peace. When you hear that harmonious resonance of the Spirit in the group you are ready to move forward. When successes result from the decision, everyone celebrates. When challenges arise, everyone faces it together. If there is no peace in a decision, then go back to the beginning, wait and pray.

LISTEN WITH THE HEART
(sourced from *The 9 Arts of Having Spiritual Conversations* by Mary Schaller and John Crilly)

So, you've been noticing the people around you and making **Level 1 Contacts,** you've been praying for your **Two Plus** people, you've moved into **Level 2 Contact** opening your heart to love and welcome. Along the way you may even be serving together at the *Live the Love* Pack event or sharing tools and tips around the house. One more skill is essential when you start asking questions and having getting-to-know-you conversations, you must listen with the heart.

Your "new" friend is feeling safer in your relationship and you hear of some tragedy or struggle, past or present and you freeze. What can you possibly say? Listen some more! Empathy offers comfort not solutions. Listen to understand the person's experience and feelings. Ask "How are you?" "What are you going through?" and give them time while you keep quiet and listen. Use a couple phrases liberally such as "Wow!" or "That's really interesting." These reinforce your investment in their story and hampers your tendency to hijack the conversation by telling your own story. Sit back, open your ears, and allow God to control the outcome of the conversation rather than worrying about where this is all headed. If needed, ask questions that dig the relationship deeper by going for the "why," not just the "how" or "what." People are surprisingly open when you are really paying attention.

Skip the advice and ask to pray with them. You'll be surprised how often the offer is accepted! This is not a sermon disguised as a prayer. Pray what you have heard, a simple cry of their heart to God. Tell God of your confidence in his presence, mercy, and might despite the current experience and thank him ahead of time for what he is going to bring about.

PRAYER CIRCLE WALK

Never stop praying, especially for others. Always pray by the power of the Spirit. Stay alert and keep praying for God's people. Pray that I will be given the message to speak and that I may fearlessly explain the mystery about the good news. (Ephesians 6:18,19 CEV)

Relationships become circles, people linked together. Just look around the "circle" of your small group. Your relationship has gained a tighter weave during these studies as you've been praying together and for each other. We've seen in Acts how God keeps expanding the circle of the church, often by creating new ones and linking them together.

We invite you to walk a circle of prayer with your group. Simply gather, follow the route you choose, and pray as the Spirit guides you. Keep your eyes open and notice details and people in the environment and include those in your prayers.

Choosing Your Route

Your conversations during *This Is Us* may have repeatedly touched on an issue or people group or neighborhood. This is the Holy Spirit nudging, so pay attention. Consider what location may give you a good focus and new perspective to pray together. If your group has had one consistent location, like a Panera or Starbucks, you could circle it with prayer. You could circle a neighborhood, a local commercial area, a village or city hall, your workplace.

We especially invite you to circle our Trinity sites with prayer. You may choose the site your group attends, or you may choose to support the launching ministry of our two newer sites with a prayer circle. You might choose to do more than one!

General agenda:

Pray that the Holy Spirit would open your eyes and your hearts for the people in the circle you're walking.

Pray that you would see the doors that are opening.

Pray that you would be more like Jesus in this place.

Pray for the power of the Holy Spirit to fill everything we do that touches the people in this circle.

Trinity Kimberly Way
1101 Kimberly Way, Lisle, IL 60532

Include a walk through the preschool wing and the 200 wing. In addition, go outdoors and walk down Kimberly Way, south on Kingston, back up 59th Street to Route 53, and back to the south parking lot.

Pray for
- Our ministry in growing disciples (200 wing): that we would continue to help people take a next step in their walk with Christ.
- Our outreach to the community (neighborhood): this includes the Meadows, but also the broader Lisle community.
- Our ministry to the next generation (preschool wing): That TKW would be a place that really forms the next generation in the faith and serves families with young children.

Trinity Green Trails
2701 Maple Ave., Lisle, IL 60532

You can follow a route through our Grounds For Hope Café and Play Center during business hours 7am–6pm, or make arrangements with melanie.lohmeyer@tlc4u.org if you would like evening access. You could also follow a route through the Green Trails neighborhood.

Pray for
- Our ministry to all people from the community who visit Grounds for Hope and the PlayCenter (our building): that we would build deeper relationships and help people find their way back to God.
- Our outreach to the community and the Green Trails neighborhood
- The neighborhood where your group is meeting—that all of our homes would be used for sharing God's love and grace with our neighbors.

Trinity Galewood
1701 N. Narragansett Ave., Chicago, IL 60639

Contact Pastor Dave (dave.mcginley@tlc4u.org) if you want to arrange to pray on site at Trinity Galewood.

- Pray that Trinity Galewood would be a reflection of the community. That we as people would not just reflect the status or color of leadership but would rather be a community that embraces diversity in all areas of life.
- Pray for a greater understanding of the Good News of Jesus and that the Gospel would drive and motivate us as we serve our neighbor.
- Pray that walls would be broken down; that barriers that have existed would turn into bridges and that our community would be a catalyst for change instead of division with no more invisible fences that push some out but instead would include all.
- Lastly for leadership for Trinity Galewood. That leaders from the community would rise up and join in on the mission of what God is already doing.

Trinity South Naperville and Trinity Early Childhood Center
2244 W. 95th St., Suite 101, Naperville, IL 60565

For security reasons, the facility of TECC is locked while we are caring for children. You could, however, circle the parking lot or playground for a prayer walk. Evenings or weekends would be preferred. Contact cassandra.sund@tlc4u.org. Our Trinity South Naperville site is currently worshipping at Neuqua Valley Birkett Freshman Center, 3220 Cedar Glade Rd., Naperville, IL. Contact mike.curtis@tlc4u.org for the best tips on how to circle their location in prayer.

- Pray that our staff serves the children with loving hearts in a way that brings glory to God.
- Pray that our client families are drawn to Christ by the love and acceptance they find at TECC.

- Pray for leadership for Trinity South Naperville as they grow into a worshipping community.
- Pray that language barriers would be bridged to make way for the Gospel.

SIMPLE WAYS TO BE MISSIONAL
(sourced from VergeNetwork.org)

Romans 10:14 NLT
But how can they call on him to save them unless they believe in him? And how can they believe in him if they have never heard about him? And how can they hear about him unless someone tells them?
(And add... how can you tell them if you don't know them?)

Missional living is simply making a choice to get to know people, to raise the possibility of having them invite you into a conversation that will get into "God territory." If you're feeling isolated in your neighborhood or workplace or community try one of these tactics and see what new relationship God will open.

Neighborhood
- Stay outside in the front yard longer while watering the yard.
- Walk your dog regularly around the same time in your neighborhood.
- Sit on the front porch and let kids play in the front yard.
- Do a food drive or coat drive and get neighbors involved.
- Art swap night—bring out what you're tired of and trade with neighbors.
- Grow a garden and give out extra produce to neighbors.
- Do a summer BBQ every Friday night or Saturday breakfast routine in your neighborhood and invite others to potluck.
- Start a walking/running group in the neighborhood.

Workplace
- Instead of eating lunch alone, intentionally eat with other co-workers and learn their story.
- Get to work early so you can spend some time praying for your co-workers and the day ahead.
- Make it a daily priority to speak or write encouragement when someone does good work.
- Make a list of your coworkers' birthdays and find a way to bless everyone on their birthday.
- Make every effort to avoid gossip in the office. Be a voice of thanksgiving not complaining.
- Ask someone who others typically ignore if you can grab them a soda/coffee while you're out.
- Be the first person to greet and welcome new people.
- Make every effort to know the names of co-workers and clients along with their families.
- Visit coworkers when they are in the hospital.
- Go out of your way to talk to your janitors and cleaning people who most people overlook.
- Invite your co-workers in to the service projects you are already involved in.

Community
- Be a regular—local café, pub, park, or shop to become known as a local. Learn the names of staff.
- Share your passion—Find a local group that shares your passion. Be missional and have fun at the same time!
- Walk—make your shopping visit an excuse to get in more steps around your retail center. Ask God to get your attention.
- Take the kids to story time at your local library regularly and get to know other parents and the library staff.
- Join a sports league—coach a kid's league.
- Attend your local government's "Coffee With" events and get to know the people who have a heart for your community.

READING RECOMMENDATIONS

The Generosity Ladder by Nelson Searcy

Imagine a life in which you don't struggle to make ends meet each month—a life with no debt, a healthy savings account, and solid plans for retirement. Imagine being able to help people in need and give to causes much bigger than your own concerns.

Sound impossible? It isn't. This is how God wants you to live. And it is attainable.

A first read if you want to handle your finances in a way that honors God and gives you security for the future. With the help of this practical and insightful book, you'll finally uncover your true level of financial health and discover a step-by-step plan to save, spend, and invest your money in a responsible and godly way.

Generosity Factor by Ken Blanchard

In the tradition of the bestselling book *The One Minute Manager*®, authors Ken Blanchard and S. Truett Cathy, entrepreneur and founder of Chic-fil-A® restaurants, present this parable that demonstrates the virtues of generosity.

It's the story of a meeting between the Broker—a young man on his way up the corporate ladder who has the illusion of success, yet deep inside feels insignificant—and the Executive—the CEO of a very large and successful company who claims the greatest joy in his life is his ability to give to others.

Thinking he might get a competitive edge by meeting with the Executive, the Broker's worldview is turned upside down as he talks to the Executive and hears the principles that form his life. He calls it The Generosity Factor™—a way to give time, talent, treasure, and touch to those in need.

Providing a unique twist on what it means to thrive in business, at home, and in life, this story will forever change your definition of success.

The Pursuit of God in the Company of Friends by Rich Lamb

You were not meant to walk alone.

Many of us struggle to forge deep relationships with God and other people. Modern society has isolated us as rugged individuals, deceiving us into thinking we can make it through life on our own. Individualism has likewise shaped the pattern of Christian discipleship, privatizing faith and separating us from fellow believers.

But we come to know God best when others help us on the way. And our friendships develop best when we seek after God together. What would it look like to pursue God not by ourselves but in the company of friends?

According to the model of the New Testament, spiritual transformation takes place in the context of Christian community. By unpacking the Gospel narratives of Jesus' ministry with his disciples, Richard Lamb demonstrates how discipleship develops within the shared community life of groups of Christians. He explores a range of topics—such as spiritual friendship, hospitality, leadership, service, conflict, forgiveness and mission--in light of Christian community. Engaging stories from real-life experience show how people can form one another spiritually when their lives are tumbled against one another.

If you long for more of God, deeper friendships or both, this book will help you on the journey. Discover the transforming power of discipleship in community. Join the pursuit of God in the company of friends.

Being There: How to Love Those Who are Hurting by Dave Furman

Everyone has friends or family who suffer from sickness, disability, depression, or the death of a loved one. Often times, the people who love the hurting also struggle in their own unique ways. They tend to suffer in silence and without much support from others. Writing from the unique perspective of one who needs extra help on a daily basis, Dave Furman offers insight into the support, encouragement, and wisdom that people need when helping others. Furman draws on his own life experiences, examples from the Bible, and wisdom from Christians throughout history to address the heart and ministry of those who are called to serve others. Deeply personal and powerfully pastoral, this book points readers to the strength that only God can provide as they love those who are hurting.

Joining Jesus on His Mission by Greg Finke

Joining Jesus on His Mission will alter the way you see your life as a follower of Jesus and take you beyond living your life for Jesus to living life with Jesus. Simple, powerful and applicable insights show you how to be on mission and recognize where Jesus is already at work in your neighborhoods, workplaces and schools. You will feel both relief and hope. You may even hear yourself say, "I can do this!" as you start responding to the everyday opportunities Jesus is placing in your path.

Flesh: Learning to be Human Like Jesus by Hugh Halter

If we're honest, no one really cares about theology unless it reveals a gut-level view of God's presence. According to pastor and ministry leader Hugh Halter, only the incarnational power of Jesus satisfies what we truly crave, and once we taste it, we're never the same. God understands how hard it is to be human, and the incarnation—God with us—enables us to be fully alive. With refreshing, raw candor, *Flesh* reveals the faith we all long to experience—one based on the power of Christ in the daily grind of work, home, school, and life. For anyone burned out, disenchanted, or seeking a fresh honest-to-God encounter, *Flesh* will invigorate your faith.

The Neighboring Church: Getting Better at What Jesus Says Matters Most by Brian Mavis and Rick Rusaw

In the parable of the Good Samaritan, the person in need doesn't get any help until somebody gets off their donkey. This book demystifies the practice of being a neighbor so we can actually live out Jesus' command to love our neighbors.

***The 9 Arts of Having Spiritual Conversations: Walking Alongside People Who Believe Differently* by Mary Schaller and John Crilly**

Could evangelism really be as simple as loving God and loving others? Navigating loaded questions and different perspectives can be scary, difficult and uncomfortable. Imagine if Christians simply spent time with people who are far from God and provided a safe place to talk about spiritual matters. What if we listened as Jesus did?

SMALL GROUPS IN PLANNING CENTER

Instructions for the Small Group Leaders

Introduction

Starting this Fall, we are using a new platform to help people join small groups as well as allow leaders to keep their members connected and up-to-date. The platform is called Planning Center Groups (https://planning.center/groups/). Through Planning Center Groups, you will be able to:

- Post information about your group (where you meet, when, and at what time)
- Schedule events
- Email members
- Share resources

But the first step in starting this process is to set up your group...

Setting Up Your Group

To set up your group, you need to contact one of the coaches at your location (see section Who Is My Coach?) and give them the following information:

- Group Name (Ex: Price "This is US" Small Group)
- The names of your leaders
- Day, Time, and Location that your group will be meeting
- What the start date for your group is

Your coach may have other questions for you as well, like "Does your group provide childcare?" or "Are rides available for members who need them?"

Answering these questions promptly will ensure your group is set up quickly and accurately so that people can easily search for and join your group.

Important Note: Your group will not go "live" until we have that information. So if you want to start using Groups and having people sign up, you need to get that info to us ASAP.

Once your group is set up, you will receive a confirmation email in your inbox, with a link to your group page. You can then go to the group page and start editing and modifying all your info so that it is as current as possible.

WHO IS MY COACH?

That's a great question! Here are the coaches for each site:

Trinity Galewood
- Zach Gates (zach.gates@tlc4u.org)

Trinity Green Trails
- Tony Dieckmann (tony.dieckmann@tlc4u.org)
- Dan Grissom (dan.grissom@tlc4u.org)

Trinity Kimberly Way
- Dennis Franzen (dennis.franzen@tlc4u.org)
- Nick Price (nick.price@tlc4u.org)

Trinity South Naperville
- Mike Curtis (mike.curtis@tlc4u.org)

They will help you set up your group, answer questions you have about using Planning Center Groups, and offer other kinds of leadership support to you as you work through the small group material.

USING PLANNING CENTER GROUPS ON A WEEKLY BASIS

There are a couple of important things you should do each week using Planning Center Groups. Here are three key things to make sure you are doing:

1. **Set up your small group events on your group page.**
   You need to make sure that you schedule each group session in your Groups calendar. This allows your group members to know when you ARE and when you ARE NOT meeting. They can also subscribe to the calendar through Google, iCal, Yahoo, or Outlook, so that any changes you make are automatically updated in their own personal calendars. It's a great way to ensure that no one misses a session.

2. **Take attendance**
   Each week you will receive an email asking you to take attendance for that week's session. Just click on the link in the email. It will take you to a roster of your group, and you can easily check in those who were in attendance that week. Again, it is a great way to let us know who is regularly involved in a group and it keeps you up to date on who is there regularly and who might be missing.

3. **Email reminders and updates**
   Be sure to regularly communicate with your group members. This may mean sending a group email before your next meeting with a preview of what to expect. Or maybe you follow up a session with an encouraging reminder. You can use your Group page to send emails to the whole group or specific individuals.

FURTHER TRAINING

We want to make sure you have the resources you need to succeed.

In the "Resources" tab on your group page you, as a leader, will have access to several training videos to help you prep individual studies. These videos are brief (4–5 mins) and will give you the best tips for how to prep your group sessions. There is also a training video on how to use Planning Center Groups to get the most out of the platform.

Finally, your coaches are here to help resource you as well as offer support and additional training as needed.

Made in the USA
Lexington, KY
27 September 2017